Twayne's English Authors Series

EDITOR OF THIS VOLUME

Kinley Roby

Northeastern University

Mary Lavin

TEAS 239

MARY LAVIN

By RICHARD F. PETERSON
Southern Illinois University

TWAYNE PUBLISHERS
A DIVISION OF G. K. HALL & CO., BOSTON

Library of Congress Cataloging in Publication Data

Peterson, Richard F
   Mary Lavin

   (Twayne's English authors series ; TEAS 239)
   Bibliography: p. 165 - 67
   Includes index.
   1.   Lavin, Mary, 1912 -   —Criticism and interpretation.
PR6023.A914Z83   823',9'12   78 - 329
ISBN 0 - 8057 - 6707 - X

Frontispiece photo of Mary Lavin
by Horst Tappe

For Anita

Contents

About the Author

Richard F. Peterson is an associate professor of English at Southern Illinois University. He has published studies of Joyce and O'Casey and has delivered papers at the International James Joyce Symposium and the Sean O'Casey Festival. He has also published widely on such writers as D. H. Lawrence, William Faulkner, John Steinbeck, T. S. Eliot, and Robert Graves.

Professor Peterson has taught at Southern Illinois University since 1969. He has served as Director of Undergraduate Studies and in 1977 was awarded one of the College of Liberal Arts' Outstanding Teaching Awards. He completed his dissertation in 1969 at Kent State University under the directorship of Bernard Benstock, the internationally recognized Joyce authority.

Preface

Mary Lavin's short stories have appeared in the *New Yorker*, the *Atlantic Monthly*, the *Southern Review*, and many other prestigious magazines, and subsequently have been collected into nine volumes of short stories over the past four decades. She has also written two long novels during her career.

Unfortunately, there has been little critical attention given to her work. Though Mary Lavin has been compared favorably to O'Flaherty, O'Connor, and O'Faolain, she has yet to receive serious attention as a major contributor to the art of the Irish short story. Though in recent years she has been honored by American and Irish societies for her outstanding work in literature, except for Zack Bowen's *Mary Lavin* in the Irish Writers Series, she has not been the subject of a full-length critical study.

The following work is an attempt to examine Mary Lavin's fiction in the chronological order in which the collections have appeared. The value of this approach is that it establishes the major themes and techniques of her fiction, while revealing the significant changes in her art that have taken place over the decades. Because so many of her early collections are out of print and unavailable to the reader, too often her stories are read in later editions which contain samplings from her earlier work. Thus the reader fails to observe the finely developed patterns of Mary Lavin's art which clearly emerge out of a chronological reading of her fiction. This study, then, attempts a close reading of the individual stories and a careful examination of the significance of the stories within the context of Mary Lavin's career.

Mary Lavin began her career with a commitment to writing the kind of story that allows the reader to experience the emotional reality of a character's life. She achieved this goal by narrating her stories from the perspective of her central character and revealing the emotional drama of that character's life through a clash of opposed sensibilities, often between husband and wife or mother and daughter. In the middle of her career, she turned to writing patterned stories which rely upon physical events, surprise endings, and intrusive narrators for their effectiveness, but she eventually returned to her impressionistic form and wrote powerful studies of widowhood in her later stories. Her stories in recent years have also reflected an increasing occupation with autobiographical materials.

During her career, Mary Lavin's major theme has been the terrible suffering caused by loneliness, memory, and death. Her characters often reveal the emptiness of their lives through the memory of some bitter disappointment or lost opportunity. She has successfully developed this theme in a group of short stories and novellas about the same family or character. Her five Grimes-family stories represent her most thorough and compelling study of the buried emotional life of the Irish middle class. Her Vera Traske stories reveal her sustained effort in her later career to include all the mere complexities of life into a philosophy acknowledging the potential for both tragedy and happiness in human experience.

RICHARD F. PETERSON

Southern Illinois University

Acknowledgments

I am grateful to many people for their generous help and encouragement. Zack Bowen, Chairman of the English Department of the University of Delaware, was extremely helpful in making material available as were the library staffs at the State University of New York at Binghamton and Southern Illinois University at Carbondale. I wish to acknowledge a special debt of gratitude to Alan Cohn, Humanities Librarian at Southern Illinois University, for suggesting the present study and offering support and advice for the work in progress. I also want to thank Lori Castleman for her work on the rough draft of the study, and especially Pauline Duke for her dedicated work in typing the final manuscript.

Finally, I wish to express my profound gratitude to Mary Lavin and her husband, Michael Scott, for being so kind and generous to me during my visit at the Abbey Farm, Bective. Their willingness to discuss the details of my opening biographical chapter and point out its errors and misconceptions was vital to this study. Their patience and generosity in discussing the critical views expressed in the middle chapters greatly reinforced my faith in the direction of my work. As I was leaving Bective, I felt that I had experienced a rare moment in my professional life. The warm memories that I still have of my visit to Bective remind me constantly that I also gained a great deal personally from my conversations with Mary Lavin and Michael Scott.

Chronology

1946 with the money from Mary Lavin's inheritance. *The House in Clewe Street* is published in book form.

1946 Publication of *The Becker Wives and Other Stories.*

1947 Publication of *At Sallygap and Other Stories.*

1950 Publication of *Mary O'Grady,* Mary Lavin's second and final novel.

1951 Publication of *A Single Lady and Other Stories.*

1953 Birth of third daughter, Caroline. William Walsh becomes seriously ill and withdraws his candidacy for the Dail Eireann.

1954 Death of William Walsh.

1956 Publication of *The Patriot Son and Other Stories.*

1957 Publication of *A Likely Story,* Mary Lavin's first book-length children's story.

1958 Publication of "The Living" in the *New Yorker.* Mary Lavin becomes a regular contributor to the magazine over the next two decades.

1959 Publication of *Selected Stories.* Mary Lavin's "Preface" is her only published essay on the art of her fiction. Receives first Guggenheim award. Asks for a renewal, which she receives for 1960 - 61.

1961 Publication of *The Great Wave and Other Stories.* Mary Lavin is awarded the Katherine Mansfield Prize for "The Great Wave."

1964 Publication of *The Stories of Mary Lavin.*

1967 Publication of *In the Middle of the Fields.* Writer-in-residence at the University of Connecticut, Storrs. Returns to position in 1971.

1968 Mary Lavin is awarded the Honorary Doctor of Literature from University College, Dublin.

1969 Marries Michael Scott after he receives laicization from the Jesuit Order. Publication of *Happiness and Other Stories.* Death of Nora Lavin.

1971 Publication of *Collected Stories,* with an introduction by V. S. Pritchett. Begins first of two terms as president of the Irish Academy of Writers.

1972 Publication of *The Second Best Children in the World.* Receives Ella Lynam Cabot Award.

1973 Publication of *A Memory and Other Stories.* Appearance of the autobiographical story "Tom" in the *New Yorker.*

1975 Awarded the Eire Society Medal and the Gregory Medal.

CHAPTER 1

From Athenry to Bective:
The Common Materials of Art

M ARY Lavin's life and career have little in common with
the gospel of the Irish writer according to James Joyce.
Joycean gospel has it that the Irish writer spends his early years
struggling against repressive nationalistic and religious forces. At
some crucial moment in his life, he experiences an epiphany, leaves
Ireland, and spends the rest of his life in rebellious exile. Once he
follows the path of Ireland's celebrated Wild Geese, he writes about
the atmosphere and conditions which he found so intolerable. What
adds even greater dimension to this story of the Irish writer is that it
blends well with the myth of the Irish political leader who serves his
people only to be betrayed by his followers. With ample historical
evidence that Ireland is the old sow that eats her farrow, the Irish
writer, faced with the likely prospect of suffering the fate of Edward
Fitzgerald, Robert Emmet, Wolfe Tone, or Charles Parnell, prefers
to sacrifice his genius to art rather than unappreciative and deadly
Ireland.

Though Mary Lavin is often mentioned with her fellow Irish
writers Liam O'Flaherty, Sean O'Faolain, and Frank O'Connor, her
life breaks the pattern of the modern Irish writer. Though not born
in Ireland, she enjoyed her school years at an Irish convent, suffered
no humiliation, and loved the nuns. She also had a great love and
respect for her father, later creating warm and sympathetic portraits
of him in some of her stories. As an observer of Irish life, she seldom
treats the nationalistic themes traditionally associated with Irish fiction. Only one of her early stories, "At Sallygap," traces the pattern
of moral and spiritual paralysis Joyce exposed with scrupulous
meanness in *Dubliners*. "The Patriot Son," her only story dealing
with Ireland's political turmoil, is mostly occupied with the
problems of a shopkeeper's son in overcoming his mother's domina-

15

tion. There are bad priests in Mary Lavin's fiction, like the insensitive Father Gogarty in "A Wet Day" and the miserly canon in "A
Pure Accident," but they are balanced by the kindly and generous
priests in "The Pastor of Six Mile Bush" and "Happiness." When
asked once if she felt herself a part of the tradition of Irish
literature, Mary Lavin answered that since she lived in Ireland most
of her life, her raw material was Irish, but she was not aware of being a particularly Irish writer: "Anything I wanted to achieve was in
the traditions of world literature. I did not read the Irish writers until I had already dedicated myself to the short story. . . . O'Connor, O'Faolain, and O'Flaherty were only a part of literature as I
saw it."[1]

   Mary Lavin did not live in Ireland until she was nearly ten years
old. She was born in East Walpole, Massachusetts, on June 11,
1912.[2] Her father, Tom Lavin, after spending his childhood in
Frenchpark, County Roscommon, went to America when he was
still young. On a return trip to Ireland to buy some horses for the
firm that employed him in America, he met Nora Mahon, the
woman he was to marry three years later. Nora, the daughter of a
merchant from Athenry, County Galway, was returning to Ireland
from a visit with a cousin who lived in Massachusetts. Her father's
business was successful but its funds were constantly strained by the
demands of twelve children. Nora, the second-oldest child and the
oldest daughter, was actually invited to America by her cousin in
the hope that she would marry and remain in the country. It is also
possible that the visit was arranged by Nora's Catholic family to
break up her recent engagement to a Protestant. If so, the visit also
prevented her from entering into what the Mahons saw as a disastrous marriage. She stayed with her granduncle, the Reverend
James Dermody, pastor of the Roman Catholic Church in Waltham
and the brother of the first American killed in the Spanish-
American War. Nora quickly learned, however, that she disliked the
country. When she returned to Ireland, she had no intention of ever
living permanently in America.

   "Tom," a short story first published in 1973, is based upon Mary
Lavin's memory of the history of her parents' courtship and the
emotional climate of their marriage. What emerges from the story is
the portrait of a mixed match, a "romantic, but not happy
marriage" distinguished by the fact that the couple, despite their
contrasting natures, "kept faith with each other."[3] The actual
relationship between Mary Lavin's parents suffered from the same

inevitable clash of opposed natures and interests. Like the fictional Tom, Mary Lavin's father, a man of great physical strength, had little formal schooling. On the other hand, the real-life counterpart of the woman that caught Tom's eye "the minute he went up the gangplank" had a classical beauty enhanced by her gentle manners. After a three-year correspondence conducted more ardently by Tom Lavin, who admired Nora Mahon's refinement, than by Nora, who had reservations about Tom's ways, she decided to return to America and marry him, thereby fulfilling her obligation as the oldest daughter in the family.

Mary Lavin has written about her great love for her father throughout her career. In "Tom" she describes "the gold spikes of love with which he pierced me to the heart when I was a child."[4] In one of her earliest stories, "Say Could That Lad Be I?" she created a tender and loving portrait of Tom Lavin as a wild lad with an equally wild dog. Not only the story but the manner in which it is told expresses her father's personality and the deep devotion and respect she held for him. There are also a number of characters in Mary Lavin's fiction that have Tom as their first name. They tend to be vital, sometimes vulnerable, human beings. Though they vary in emotional strength, they are usually treated sympathetically even when they fail.

Nora Lavin has not fared as well in her daughter's fiction. Stories with mother-daughter relationships usually portray the mother as a rival rather than a confidante. The loving, long-suffering mother in *Mary O'Grady* is more a projection of ideal motherhood than a tribute to any real mother. There is no gallery of Nora characters in Mary Lavin's fiction, but the female characters that have Nora Lavin's refinement also have the same tendency to withdraw from the realities of life.

What Mary Lavin observed in her parents' marriage was the conflict possible in a relationship between opposed personalities. Nora's negative attitude toward America was reinforced rather than changed by her marriage because of her unwillingness to adjust to a life-style entirely different from the one she knew in Ireland. She never overcame her feeling that her husband's work forced her to associate with people who were her social inferiors. Even the birth of a daughter was not enough to soften her conviction to return to Ireland. She actually tried to visit her relatives during her pregnancy, and was stopped only through the warning of her doctor. Finally, after ten years in America, Nora Lavin made the decision in her

own mind to return permanently to Ireland with her daughter, even
though her husband saw it only as another one of her visits to the
Mahons.

Mary Lavin's brief association with America provided some
memories but little material for her stories. Two of her most interesting characters, Patrick from *Mary O'Grady* and Tom from
"The Little Prince," emigrate to America. They are both warm and
fun-loving characters, but they suffer terrible fates in the new country. The only story that directly reflects her early life in America is
"Lemonade." One of her most autobiographical stories,
"Lemonade" is really two stories in one. The first part of the
narrative is the story of a critical moment in the life of her mother
and father, while the second part tells the story of a sensitive and
perceptive child's first day at a new school, and her encounter with
social and emotional pressures she never knew existed.

The beginning of "Lemonade" gives a personal view of the relationship between Tom and Nora Lavin the night before she sailed
to Ireland with her daughter. The bitter feeling that has alienated
Dinny Delaney and his wife surfaces in their argument over the old
friends visiting Dinny on his last night together with his wife and
daughter. The wife's strong feeling that she has endured a way of
life socially and morally beneath her is revealed in her contempt for
her husband's cronies, her resentment of his drinking, and her bitter
disappointment that he is not returning with her to Ireland. When
her husband suggests he may buy property someday in Leitrim and
Roscommon and " 'end up in the old country,' " her scorn for Dinny's lower-class background is unmistakable: " 'Leitrim! Roscommon! I'd never have a soul to speak to from day-up to day-
down!' "5

The drama of the Delaneys' emotional conflict is played out upon
the mind of Maudie, their young daughter. Unaware of the meaning of what passes between her parents, she is caught up in the excitement of her approaching "visit" in Ireland with her aunts and
uncles. There is little reason to doubt that Mary Lavin experienced
the same enthusiasm for the trip as her fictional counterpart, but
once she settled in Athenry with her mother's people, she missed
her life in America. During the eight months Mary Lavin stayed
with the Mahons, however, the small-town life of Athenry had a
beneficial effect upon her. The new landscape, the local school, and
her aunts and uncles eventually compensated for the loss of her
home. Perhaps this is why the town itself has had such a powerful

influence upon Mary Lavin's life and career. Often a personal experience was relived as an adventure of one of her relatives. In her early career any idea for a story was usually given shape and substance from her knowledge of Athenry. As for Tom and Nora Lavin, as soon as she purchased a house in Dublin with the money her husband sent her, he returned to Ireland to join his family.

In 1922, with the family settled in Dublin, Mary Lavin was enrolled at the Loreto convent school. It was during this period of her school days in Dublin that she developed a great love for the city and a great love of books, particularly American stories. Among her early favorites were Hawthorne's *The House of the Seven Gables* and *Tanglewood Tales*. She also admired the poems of Longfellow. An only child, she read Longfellow day and night, often going out into the woods to recite his verse. She loved school, lived for the debates and plays, and excelled in athletics. She also did well in her academic work and won the Bishop's Medal for Christian Doctrine and a first place in English.

Tom Lavin's decision in 1926 to supervise the estate in County Meath purchased by his employer in America had a similar but more positive effect upon his daughter. Bective, located on the banks of the Boyne, looks out across the plains of Tara Hill. In *A Likely Story,* Mary Lavin describes its almost magical beauty: "Do you know Bective? Like a bird in the nest, it presses close to the soft green mound of the river bank, its handful of houses no more significant by day than the sheep that dot the far fields. But at night, when all its little lamps are lit, house by house, it is marked out on the hillside as clearly as the Great Bear is marked out in the sky."[6] Bective became another of the great early influences on Mary Lavin's life. By the time she finished her school years at Loreto and began her career at University College, Dublin, in 1930, she had gathered in her imagination and heart much of the material that would later be transformed into the characters and settings of her fiction.

Mary Lavin describes herself as an ordinary student, but she did well in college, particularly in her last year. She took first honors in English and second honors in French. Her French professor was especially impressed with her discriminating knowledge of French literature. During her very first day at University College, she met Michael Scott, a first-year Jesuit student who had arrived the previous night from Australia. Though they were fond of each other throughout their undergraduate years, they never pursued a personal relationship because of Michael Scott's deep feelings and commitment to the Jesuit Order.

She completed her thesis on Jane Austen in 1936; but when she submitted her work earlier than she had intended to, her academic career almost came to a disastrous end. When her father, often the tempter in the past, invited her to travel with him to America, she left a badly edited version of her thesis to be typed by a friend. When she returned a few months later, Professor Hogan, her academic director, told her that her thesis showed a great love of literature. Unfortunately, it had so many typing errors that he could not decide between a fail or first-class honors. Resisting her pleas for something between the two, Professor Hogan allowed the external examiner to make the final decision. Recognizing the intrinsic value of the thesis, the examiner gave it first-class honors.

Having survived her father's latest cavalier gesture toward formal education, Mary Lavin began work on her Doctor of Philosophy degree. In the next two years, she taught French at the Loreto convent school and prepared for her degree. All during the period leading up to her work on her dissertation, she continued to develop her great love for reading into a deeper and deeper appreciation of literature. She never felt, however, the ambition to write fiction. She was in college at a time when many of her contemporaries were already writing, but she thought of their work as a supplement to their academic life. She possessed "a curious naiveté—that literature was written by the dead."[7] The selection of Virginia Woolf as her dissertation topic, however, soon brought an end to that view.

In 1938, after returning from a four-month visit to Boston, Mary Lavin suddenly turned to writing fiction. When someone spoke casually of having taken tea with Virginia Woolf, she was stirred by the comment. All during that day she wondered what Virginia Woolf was doing. Suddenly realizing that she might be at her desk writing, she finally "made the connection between the work and the hand that wrote it."[8] Turning over the typescript of her thesis, she wrote her "first story on it."[9] The story, which she called "Miss Holland," was rejected by several magazines. When, however, she sent it to Seumas O'Sullivan, the editor of *Dublin Magazine,* her luck changed and her work began to attract public and critical recognition.

Seumas O'Sullivan and Lord Dunsany were the early catalysts in Mary Lavin's literary career. O'Sullivan, the first editor to recognize her work, was responsible for publishing her first story in the April-June 1939 issue of *Dublin Magazine*. Impressed by the "delicate restraint" of "Miss Holland," he agreed to consider any other verse or prose that she might like to send him.[10] Subsequently, two poems and two other short stories, "Say Could That Lad Be I?" and "A Fable," appeared during the next two years in *Dublin Magazine*. After reading "Miss Holland," Lord Dunsany also offered his help in bringing her stories to the notice of editors. He became a great admirer of Mary Lavin's stories, comparing their truthfulness to the realism of Russian fiction. He was also responsible for the first appearance of her work in America. Through Lord Dunsany's recommendation, *Atlantic Monthly* published "The Green Grave and the Black Grave" in 1940 and "At Sallygap" in 1941. He also advised her on the arrangement of her stories for their publication in book form. When the collection of stories, significantly named *Tales from Bective Bridge*, was published in 1942, it had a preface written by Lord Dunsany. Though his letters to her show that he encouraged her to read O'Henry and strengthen her plots, he states in the preface that he had nothing to teach her about literature. His only function is to "stand as it were, at the portals of this book to point within to what you may find for yourselves, and to recommend you to look for it."[11]

At the beginning of her literary career, Mary Lavin started another career that often deprived her of the time she wanted for her writing. In 1942, she married William Walsh, whom she had met at University College, Dublin. By the time of the marriage, he had become a lawyer and had developed his practice in Dublin. With the birth of Valentine, her first daughter, in 1943 and Elizabeth in 1945, Mary Lavin's family responsibilities increased to the point that she had to steal the time from other duties to complete her writing. Though she managed to write two novels, *The House in Clewe Street* and *Mary O'Grady*, she soon discovered that the intensity and brevity of the short story best suited her personality and needs. In 1945, she lost her beloved father. His death brought to an end the single greatest influence on her life. She was deeply moved by her father's death. She once wrote that death is sad only when it ends beauty or joy.[12] As her stories clearly show, she retained the memories of the beauty and joy of her life with Tom Lavin as some compensation for his death.

With the money from her inheritance, Mary Lavin and her husband decided to buy the Abbey Farm in Bective. In the next several years the family divided its time between Bective and Dublin, where William Walsh had his legal practice. The Abbey Farm increased the family duties, which seriously limited Mary Lavin's opportunities for writing. Months sometimes passed before she could return to her writing. At times, she thought with some bitterness that if she stopped writing it would be "months, even years," before anyone in her family would notice "—if they ever did!"[13] Nevertheless, because of her deep belief that her writing was her life and the rest only an echo, she managed to find time for her stories. She continued to publish her work in Irish, English, and American magazines. In the next several years, from 1944 to 1951, she had four new collections of her stories published.

In 1953, Mary Lavin gave birth to her third daughter, Caroline, but she also had to face the declining health of her husband, who was suffering from heart trouble. When he died in 1954, she did not see how she could survive her emotional and practical situation. Confronted with the grim prospect of raising three young children by herself and running a farm, she developed a terrible insecurity about life and a brief uncertainty about her writing. Edward Weeks, the literary reviewer for *Atlantic Monthly*, visited Mary Lavin a few times just before the death of William Walsh. Seeing the difficult problems that existed for her before her husband's death, he wondered how she would ever find time for writing after her tragic loss and the new burdens facing her.[14] For the next several years, she managed to struggle against her despondency and survive her personal difficulties, but her literary career came to a painful halt.

Besides Mary Lavin's own resiliency and devotion to literature, the *New Yorker* and the Guggenheim Foundation had the most to do with renewing her confidence in her work. In 1958, with the contribution of a short story, "The Living," to the *New Yorker*, she began a long and rewarding relationship with the magazine. Between 1958 and 1966, she published eleven stories in the *New Yorker*, and she continued to be a regular contributor to the magazine during the 1970s. An even more important stimulus to her career was the Guggenheim award that she received for 1959 - 60. She did make a personal and financial error by using the money to take her family to Florence. The Guggenheim, however, was not wasted because it restored Mary Lavin's confidence in her work. When she returned to Ireland, she asked for a renewal, which she received, for 1960 - 61. This time she stayed at home. While her children ran and played in the fields, she wrote most of the stories for her finest collection of stories, *In the Middle of the Fields*. Only after she completed her writing did she venture abroad with her girls on a camping trip in Greece.

After William Walsh's death, Mary Lavin wrote to Michael Scott, an ordained priest since 1940. They had written to each other regularly until her marriage to William Walsh. From his residence in Australia, where he had developed an outstanding academic career in administration, he became the family's spiritual, financial, and emotional adviser. Eventually, "Father Hugh," the name she gave him in "Happiness," an autobiographical short story, filled the emptiness left by the deaths of Tom Lavin and William Walsh. In 1969, after receiving laicization, Michael Scott returned to Ireland, and he and Mary Lavin were married. The decade which began with her Guggenheim awards and ended with her marriage reversed the pattern of creative uncertainty and personal tragedy that had haunted Mary Lavin in the 1950s. The widow stories written during the period of her second Guggenheim take their power from her ability to objectify her own emotional ordeals.

The 1960s also saw an increase in public recognition and honors. At the beginning of her career, she had received the James Tait Black Memorial Book Prize for *Tales from Bective Bridge*. In 1961, she was awarded the Katherine Mansfield Prize for "The Great Wave." In 1967, she was writer-in-residence at the University of Connecticut, Storrs, and returned in 1971 for a similar assignment. During that time, she read at several American universities, including Vassar, Kenyon, Bryn Mawr, Boston College, and the University of Pennsylvania. In 1968, University College, Dublin, made her an Honorary Doctor of Literature.

The only significant shift in Mary Lavin's career in recent years has been a tendency to write stories of an autobiographical nature. "Villa Violetta" is based on her frantic experiences with her children in Florence, while "Tom" is a tender tribute to her father. Out of her widow stories she created an autobiographical heroine, Vera Traske. Her autobiographical stories, however, exhibit the same strong themes and controlled narrative of her best fiction. Her work has received additional honors in the 1970s. She received the Ella Lynam Cabot Award in 1972. In 1975 she was honored with the Eire Society Medal (previous winners had been Siobhan McKenna and John F. Kennedy) and the Gregory Medal, which Yeats described as the supreme award of the Irish nation for writers of literature. She also served two terms as president of the Irish

Academy of Writers from 1971 - 75. She still lives at the Abbey Farm in Bective, but the family also has a house in Dublin, where Michael Scott is presently the director of the School of Irish Studies.

Of all her stories, "Happiness" stands out as the strongest expression of the philosophy that sustained Mary Lavin through her joyous and tragic seasons. Curiously, Vera, her autobiographical heroine, dies in the story. Told from the perspective of one of her children, "Happiness" reveals Vera's unwavering belief in the value of life. For Vera, this world remains the right place for love. Like the speaker in Robert Frost's "Birches," she does not know where it is likely to go better. Considering the family tragedies and the loving memories, the personal disappointments and the joyful moments of creation, Mary Lavin's own life and career best exemplify the narrative description in "Happiness" of the source of Vera's enduring strength: "You see, annoyance and fatigue, according to Mother, and even illness and pain, could coexist with happiness."[15]

More than any other modern poet, William Butler Yeats believed that life runs its course between extremities. Mary Lavin also has been keenly aware of life's eternal conflicts. She has offered her readers story after story that radiate the tenderness and tragedy she has observed and experienced as the constant source of her own happiness.

CHAPTER 2

The Early Stories: The Drama of Opposed Sensibilities

IN the three collections of stories published in the 1940s, Mary Lavin established the emotional drama and technical strategy of her art. In story after story, the emotional ordeal of her characters is created out of the clash of opposed interests and sensibilities. Because of their radically different natures, her characters, husband-wife, mother-daughter, fail to see beyond their own narrow viewpoint. The tragic result is the failure of one human being to understand the emotional needs of another. By narrating her stories from the point of view of her more sensitive and introverted characters, Mary Lavin also reveals how human beings of delicate sensibility risk their souls when encountering those less sensitive and perceptive in nature. If they shun contact with the coarser side of life, however, these characters risk denying themselves the chance to participate fully in life's feast. Gradually emerging out of these early stories, then, is the portrait of an Irish middle class peopled by lonely, sometimes bitter characters trapped by their own natures and their frustrated emotional needs. Within this portrait, Mary Lavin's characters act out their own individual failures or discover the terrible emptiness of their lives.

I Tales from Bective Bridge

"At Sallygap" holds a unique position in the Lavin canon. It was one of her first stories published in America, appeared in her first collection of short stories, and became the title story of a collection published four years after *Tales from Bective Bridge*. It was also included in *Collected Stories* and *The Stories of Mary Lavin*. Robert W. Caswell, writing in the late 1960s, regarded "At Sallygap" as Mary Lavin's "only full-scale rendering to date of the familiar

25

pattern of paralysis, decay, and spiritual death in Irish life with exile
as the only ready solution."[1] The pattern Caswell describes is particularly striking in the opening moments of the story. In temperament and situation, Manny Ryan belongs to the gallery of lost Irish
souls James Joyce exposed in *Dubliners*. In his frustrated, pathetic
yearnings and his dull, loveless marriage, Manny resembles Little
Chandler of "A Little Cloud."[2] In his failure before his marriage to
seize an opportunity to escape Dublin, he shares the fate of the
young girl in "Eveline." When he finally discovers there is no sanctuary from the emptiness of his present life, he undergoes the same
terrible awakening that comes to several adult characters in
Dubliners, particularly James Duffy in "A Painful Case" and
Gabriel Conroy in "The Dead."

Much of the early part of "At Sallygap" has to do with Manny
Ryan's memory of his lost opportunity to leave Dublin when he was
a young man playing the fiddle in the Mary Street Band. Excited by
a rare trip into the country and the sight of the mail boat on its way
to England, he tells a young man sitting beside him of the band's
decision to make its fortune in "gay Paree" and of his own last-
minute decision to remain in Dublin because he felt an obligation to
his wife, Annie. He also explains how his effort to retrieve his fiddle
from the departing mail boat was thwarted when the fiddle was
tossed against an iron stump and smashed into small pieces. The
memory of his abortive dream of adventure and the present reality
of his shopkeeper's existence create such an uncommon state of excitement in Manny's mind that he offers advice to the young man
which comes too late for those who learn its truth and too soon for
those who are still capable of acting: " 'Clear out and go.
. . . That's what I'd say to you if you were my own son. Cut and
run for it!' "[3]

The importance of "At Sallygap" extends far beyond the familiar
Irish theme of spiritual paralysis, for the story also develops several
of the basic techniques of Mary Lavin's fiction. She often reveals
the emotional reality of her characters by moving them from a fixed
point in time, uneventful in itself, to a moment in the past which
exposes the painful truth of their lives. At the same time, the oppressiveness of one memory, heavily weighted with emotional content, often denies her characters the chance to express their feelings
through some dramatic statement or action. At the most, the typical
Lavin story offers a brief glimpse of the truth without suggesting
any conclusion or remedy for the conditions of her characters.

Another common strategy evident in "At Sallygap" is the use of one symbol to reveal the buried emotions of her characters. Manny's smashed fiddle symbolizes the end of his hope for escape and adventure; but because Manny remembers the minor tragedy as he travels into the country in search of a distributor of fresh eggs, the fragments of his fiddle also symbolize the chaos of his married life.

Because the opening moments of "At Sallygap" concentrate so effectively on the emotional paralysis of the Irish middle class, the full significance of the second half of the story is easily overlooked. Besides its important techniques, "At Sallygap" also has the type of relationship that several critics have identified as the basic emotional situation of Mary Lavin's most successful stories.[4] Though her characters almost always represent the commonplace world of shopkeepers, farmers, laborers, and servant girls, she conveys the full truth of their lives through a clash of sensibilities. Augustine Martin finds in her stories "a whole range of characters who recoil from the more fullblooded implications of life and settle for a cool cloistered compromise; over against them stands an equal rank of figures who are characterized by their energetic commitments to the hot realities of life."[5] Others see the conflict more in terms of the contrast between sensitive characters hoping for love and beauty in their lives and insensitive characters seeking their fulfillment within the social and economic conventions of the Irish middle class.[6]

In "At Sallygap" the emotional incompatibility between Manny and Annie Ryan exposes their unhappiness and loneliness. Sensitive and artistic by nature, Manny, during his rare day in the country, experiences a richness and beauty that awakens his mind. In his discovery of the "potent beauty" of nature, he revives "some dim green corner of his mind" (p. 110) which reasserts itself against the sordidness of Dublin. As he approaches the city, he actually believes for the moment he has found a real escape from his narrow and bleak existence: "There are gentle souls who take nothing from their coarse rearing and less from their chance schooling, but who yet retain their natural gentleness, and sometimes it flowers, as Manny's did, in the hills" (p. 111).

Manny's gentleness, however, lacks strength; and nature is no cure-all for a weak human nature. Once he enters the city, his old fears return as the painful truth of his life once again forms around him. As Manny's brief adventure ends, however, the narrative perspective shifts to Annie Ryan. While Manny's shriveled soul has struggled for flight against those hard Joycean realities, Annie's soul has also been soaring. She is the full-blooded character, described by Martin, who seeks "the hot realities of life." For her, marriage was to be an escape from monotony. What she discovered was an emotional blind alley, a "greater boredom" than she had ever known before. Manny's complacency is her curse. Her fierce nature, thwarted by the weakness of his gentleness and kindness, seeks in rage what it fails to find in the marriage bed. When her emasculated husband does not return at his usual time, Annie imagines that the violent life she has experienced vicariously in the gossip of her customers now awaits her. Her thoughts and emotions range from the excitement of jealousy to the terror of death—but Manny's footfall ends all speculation. As the narrative perspectives merge, the truth of the situation becomes painfully clear. Manny's brief dream of escape falters in a soul so timid it cannot assert itself even in the face of degradation. His only epiphany is the trembling discovery that Annie's nature, so twisted by frustration and anger, may one day act out its growing hatred. Manny's "terrible adult fear" as he watches Annie's "sullen malevolent eyes" (p. 122) is all that remains of their relationship. As he tries to recall something Annie said to him in the moment of her most intense rage, all his earlier thoughts fade into forgetfulness. What Manny fails to remember is a comment that he knows "was true, whatever it was" (p. 122). The one true statement, too painful to be remembered, sums up Manny's pitiful state and the source of Annie's bitterness and anger: " 'It's a queer thing when a man disgusts to himself' " (p. 121).

The emotional struggle between characters of different sensibilities is the key to theme and structure in *Tales From Bective Bridge*. In five stories Lavin offers variations on the characters and theme in "At Sallygap," but "Love Is for Lovers" follows the same basic pattern. Mathew Simmins and Rita Cooligan closely resemble Manny and Annie Ryan, even though their relationship never advances beyond the courtship stage. Shy and cautious by nature, Mathew Simmins is hardly a match for a strong and aggressive woman like Rita Cooligan once she sets her cap for him. Settled into the routine of a shopkeeper's existence at the "noncommittal age of forty-four" (p. 123), Mathew suddenly finds himself captivated by a sensuous woman embodying all those "hot realities" he had carefully avoided in the past. Their romance almost overwhelms him until he discovers that he prefers "the coldness and darkness of death" to "the hot rays of life" (p. 151). Lacking Manny Ryan's sensitive nature, Mathew Simmins becomes a far less sympathetic character when he decides to withdraw to "his chill, white bed" (p. 152). Mathew's escape from a designing and smothering woman is no alternative to the dreadful marriage in "At Sallygap." Love is for lovers of life, and Mathew, like Duffy in Joyce's "A Painful Case," has long denied himself life's feast. Unlike Joyce's bilious Dubliner, however, Mathew suffers no remorse and experiences no epiphany. Retreating from life, he now awaits "death as the next important step and it was through sweet cemetery grasses, over cold gravestones" (p. 152).

In "Lilacs" and "Sarah" the difference in sensibilities instigates the emotional conflict of the stories. There are, however, important variations in character and setting that distinguish these stories from "At Sallygap" and "Love Is for Lovers." The most interesting and sympathetic characters have a warmth and spontaneity that reflect the vitality of the Irish countryside. On the surface Phelim Molloy of "Lilacs" seems coarse and unfeeling because he deals in horse dung. He refuses to listen to his family's pleas to end the business and rid the farm of its terrible odor. The dunghill's effect upon the family, however, reveals the natural strength and goodness of Phelim and the emotional weaknesses of his wife and daughters. Unlike the passionate but insensitive characters associated with the city in "At Sallygap" and "Love Is for Lovers," Phelim possesses an intuitive understanding of life which unifies and sustains the diverse elements of his family. After Phelim's death, the dunghill takes on a symbolic power as great as its odor. Ros, his wife, spends the short time before her own death carrying on the dunghill business in homage to the memory of her husband's powerful and sensitive love. The daughters, Kate and Stacy, lack Ros's understanding of Phelim's true strength, and inherit only a part of their father's character. Kate comprehends the forcefulness of her father, but lacks his intuitive feeling for life. She keeps the dunghill because of its financial advantages. Stacy, who wants to replace the dunghill with lilac bushes, has her father's touch of the poet but lacks his powerful vision. Her vulnerability to life exposes her to the poten-tial tragedy of the weak, sensitive soul even though her fate in the story remains unknown. In other stories, the Stacy characters actual-ly approach tragic stature, while the Kates often become the unfeel-ing catalysts for their tragedies.

"Sarah" draws out the contrast between the central character's vitality and the moral and social values of the village community. A strong and tireless worker and the mother of three healthy, illegitimate children, Sarah resembles Benjamin Franklin's Polly Baker in her too-generous nature and her willingness to assume the simple virtues of country life if she can find a man to do the honorable thing. Even though the villagers condemn her lack of conventional morality, they admire her vitality and her generous heart. Unfortunately, Sarah does not share the happy fate of Polly Baker. Despite her natural goodness, she is destroyed by the moral righteousness of the "anemic and thin-boned" Kathleen Kedrigan, the moral cowardice of Kathleen's husband, Oliver, and the cruel insensitivity of her own brothers. Her pregnancy, a direct result of her brief stay as housekeeper at the Kedrigans', enhances Sarah's beauty. She carries the child with "a strange primitive grace in her rounded figure" (p. 60). Yet, while Sarah accepts childbearing without resentment, she is condemned and rejected by those who have taken advantage of her in the past, but cannot rise above their own petty fears and interests once they discover her pregnancy.

The dramatic irony of Sarah's death in a roadside ditch with the dead child beside her is that Kathleen Kedrigan, the weakest and most conventional character in the story, is to blame for the situation leading to Sarah's pregnancy. Later, she sets in motion the events which force Sarah's brothers to turn her out of the house. Through the careful manipulation of key symbols and scenes, Mary Lavin actually creates psychological doubles out of Kathleen and Sarah. Both pregnant by Oliver, they represent the emotional extremes of womanhood. Kathleen, though anemic and afraid of life, is the publicly respectable wife, deriving a perverse strength from public opinion and her own moral self-righteousness. Sarah, though condemned by the community and her family, is the natural lover, always seeking a warm and intimate relationship with life. Sarah's death, instigated by Kathleen, represents a triumph for the community, but it is the triumph of the unnatural over the natural, the perversely conventional over the independent-minded. When Kathleen tells Oliver that Sarah is dead, she is handing him the same sheep-raddle that Sarah had given Oliver as a promise of love. Now associated with death, the raddle sharply draws into focus the bitter irony of Oliver's escape from responsibility and the terrible truth of the respectable Kathleen's victory over the immoral Sarah.

"Sarah" falls short of tragedy because plot takes on more importance than character. While the chain of events leading inextricably to Sarah's death is carefully narrated, the characters are rarely more than one-dimensional representatives of distinct and limited attitudes toward life. The reader has the opportunity to judge the rigid moral attitudes which destroy Sarah, but at the end of the story he knows little of Sarah's own feelings and thoughts. In "Brother Boniface" and "A Fable," the storyteller becomes the fabulist, as the latter title obviously indicates, and the characters remain one-dimensional. "Brother Boniface" is the story of a young, sensitive lad whose poetic nature is never understood or appreciated by his parents or his religious brothers. All that Barney wants out of life is the chance to observe the holy wonders of nature. His search leads him from "the gross of tawdry coins and the gaudy pattern of bank notes" (p. 83) of his father's shopkeeper's existence to the quiet and sheltered life of the monastery. Unfortunately, his belief that once within the walls he will have ample time to appreciate God's universe is never realized. His disappointment comes early when he discovers that the young monk he watched with his face "turned upwards to the stars" had his eyes closed to the heavens while he said his office. Brother Boniface's death, after long years of service to the order, inspires the younger monks to emulate his industry, but the gentle irony of the story lies in the inside knowledge that the secret soul of the sensitive poet or the gentle lover of nature finds no chance for expression in either the secular or religious life.

"A Fable" is an interesting variation on the theme of "Brother Boniface." Told in a manner that places even less emphasis upon individual characterization, "A Fable" narrates the effect of great beauty upon common humanity. When a young woman of flawless beauty arrives in the village, she provokes resentment and hostility. Only when her face is scarred in a riding accident can the villagers appreciate her great beauty. Even after her perfect complexion is restored through plastic surgery, the people insist the scars will eventually show through the new skin. When old age finally etches faint lines on her face, those who remember the accident believe their prophecy has been fulfilled. Whereas "Brother Boniface" reveals the failure of the sensitive soul to find a place for itself in an insensitive world, "A Fable" observes the conventional response to the rare appearance of beauty so perfect and obvious in itself that it cannot be ignored. Rather than pay homage to great beauty, however, common humanity resents it, preferring to associate inner failings, like ungraciousness and immorality, with its outward perfection. Only when it can equate beauty with suffering does

humanity begin to understand and appreciate its wonder. Only
when beauty reveals itself through great tragedy does it have dignity and meaning for the human mind and soul.

In "Miss Holland," the story that began her writing career, Mary
Lavin achieves a balance between characterization and storytelling
by allowing the narrative to enter the private world of Agnes
Holland through the third-person limited point of view. The advantage of this viewpoint, which in some stories approaches the indirect
interior monologue, is that it invites the reader to experience a
character's feelings and thoughts. In the preface to *Selected Stories*,
Mary Lavin says this technique gives her reader the chance to look
"closer than normal into the human heart."[7] The narrative structure
is controlled by the central character's emotions and perceptions,
for "the vagaries and contrarieties" of the heart "have their own integral design."[8] While the content reveals what it is like to be a
human being, the form traces the secret patterns of the sensitive
heart. Thus the story achieves the delicate balance between tragedy
and beauty because it unveils the secret terror and pity of the
human soul.

Agnes Holland would fit well into a gallery of Virginia Woolf portraits. Like Clarissa Dalloway, Mrs. Ramsey, and Lily Briscoe, Miss
Holland goes through life feelingly. Told from the limited perspective Zack Bowen describes as "selective omniscience" because of its
occasional intrusiveness,[9] "Miss Holland" delicately reveals the
truth of a withdrawn, middle-aged English spinster forced to live in
a boardinghouse for the first time in her life. Faced with the hot
realities of her fellow boarders, she desperately wants to become
one of them. Her struggle, however, is never externalized until the
end of the story, when her attempt to tell a clever story at dinner
about the landlady's cat is interrupted by Mr. Moriarity, who in-
forms the company that he dispatched "that damned tomcat" with
a blast from his shotgun.

Nothing more outwardly dramatic than the embarrassing moment at the dinner table happens in "Miss Holland." And, because
of the absence of significant physical events in this story and several
others, Mary Lavin's early admirers chided her for the absence of
strong plots in her stories. The criticism, however, is as shallow as
the conversations at the dinner table on the small cost of feeding
large numbers of people, the injustice of the Rugby trials, and the
falling British birthrate. What Miss Holland fails to understand until she is rudely interrupted by Mr. Moriarity is that these subjects

serve only to hide the ugliness and smallness of her fellow boarders, that her gift, the ability to see "the small details of life that seemed to make such little impression on them" (p. 195), distinguishes rather than limits her life. She feels cheated for a time by the refined and sheltered world of books, pictures, and music inherited from her father because she cannot talk about real problems. In truth, however, she is alone because she has the sensitivity and perceptiveness to see and feel the beauty of life. Her true dilemma, and the true subject matter of the story, is whether or not she can survive in an insensitive and unfeeling world. Her desire to descend to the gross level of the boarders runs against her own nature, but her quiet rebellion against the meanness of those around her does nothing to alleviate her loneliness and isolation.

In "Miss Holland," Mary Lavin first establishes the tragic situation of her fiction. If her sensitive character attempts to reach out to those who lack feeling and awareness, she risks her own soul. If, however, she preserves her sense of beauty in the face of vulgarity and rudeness, she may deny herself a full participation in life. On the surface, Agnes Holland, because she cannot change the world of the boardinghouse, seems to symbolize the failure of the intuitive imagination. Yet, even as she withdraws from the dinner table, she accomplishes something in her own way which is as magnificent as Clarissa Dalloway's triumphant return to her party and as complete as Lily Briscoe's final stroke on her painting. Before her moment of truth, Miss Holland has always avoided ugly things by using her imagination to pretend they do not exist. Only when Mr. Moriarity destroys the one thing of beauty she experiences at the boardinghouse does she finally recognize that ugliness has its own patterns: "I must define their ugliness, their commonness, their bad taste. I must find a name for the things about them which irritate and disgust me. I can no longer delude myself" (p. 199). By refusing any longer to use her imagination to deceive herself, she can accept all levels of reality but still discriminate between those who stamp their own commonness upon life and those who perceive and appreciate life's beauty: "For a long time I tried not to notice these things. I tried to submerge them in my good opinions of these people, but now they are laid bare. Now they shall live forever in my mind. . . . Henceforth I will go consciously in the way that I have hitherto gone because my people before me went that way" (p. 199).

II   The Long Ago and Other Stories

Several stories in *The Long Ago* continue the pattern of
emotional conflict established in *Tales from Bective Bridge*, while
others reflect Mary Lavin's interest in the psychological reality of
her characters. "The Will" focuses on the clash of emotions and
economics within the Conroy family. The differences have been exposed by the mother's death and the reading of the will. Lally, the
youngest member of the family and its only black sheep, married
against her mother's wishes years ago and has since lived in near
poverty. Her exclusion from the will prompts her brother and two
sisters to insist upon a financial arrangement that will improve her
social position and erase the mistakes of the past. On the surface
their charity seems well intended, but their real concern is the embarrassment Lally's boardinghouse causes them. Stiff and conventional in behavior, Kate, Matthew, and Nonny are the respectable
Conroys, interested in the preservation and improvement of the
family's social reputation. Whatever help they offer Lally is
motivated only by their own selfishness and lack of feeling at a moment when each Conroy should be particularly vulnerable to deep
emotions and tender, loving memories of the past.

Lally's rejection of the proposal excludes her forever from the
comfortable circle of her family's social respectability and economic
security. It also, however, preserves her love and respect for her
mother and protects her basic humanity. Her only worry is protect-
ing her mother's last wishes. What she dreads facing is not her im-
poverished life but the fact that the will means her mother never
forgave her youngest daughter for marrying against her wishes. She
is afraid that her mother's soul is now in Purgatory because of the
bitterness in her heart. Ironically, she wants to use her own meager
amount of money to buy Masses for her mother. Confused by her
brief and vague impressions of Purgatory remembered from her
childhood, Lally returns to the city oblivious to her own problems
because she loves the mother who could not forgive her. She is the
only Conroy to fear and pray for a soul that damned itself by denying her own natural love for her daughter:

She leaned her head back against the cushions as the train roared into the
night, and feverishly she added the prices she would get from the tenants in
the toprooms and subtracted the amount that would be needed to buy food
for herself and the children for the week. She would have ten masses said at
least for that. . . . She tried to comfort herself by these calculations, but as

the dark train rushed through the darkness she sat more upright on the red-carpeted seats that smelled of dust and clenched her hands tightly as she thought of the torments of Purgatory. Bright red sparks from the engine flew past the carriage window; and she began to pray with rapid, unformed words that jostled themselves in her mind like sheaves of burning sparks.[10]

There are varying studies of the struggle between characters of opposed interests and sensibilities in *The Long Ago*. In "The Haymaking," Christopher Glebe, a rich farmer, surprises his neighbors by marrying a schoolteacher. Though she is excited by the prospect of her new life, Fanny Glebe has a great deal of difficulty adjusting to her husband's farming ways. Particularly oppressive is the discovery that her husband's moods, and by implication her own happiness, are dependent upon the fate of the crops. Her romantic view of nature is soon deflated by the knowledge of the realities of farming and her irreconcilable differences with her husband. In "The Long Ago," Hallie's spinsterhood separates her from Dolly and Ella, her married friends. Her failure to understand Ella's grief over her husband's death, however, is not the insensitive act of an old maid. Hallie lives so much in the past she loses emotional contact with the present lives of those around her. Like several early characters in Mary Lavin's short stories, she resembles Clarissa Dalloway in her tender memories of her girlhood. Her inability to recognize Ella's needs suggests she is trapped emotionally by her obsession with the long ago.

Death is the catalyst for conflict and alienation in "The Cemetery in the Demesne" and "Grief." In "The Cemetery in the Demesne" the presence of death alienates the central character from his family. The carter loves human companionship and the telling of a good story. His encounter with a strange, lonely woman and her dying child is so profound, however, that it isolates him from the simple pleasures of his home. His brooding silence after his journey to the demesne is completely out of character and a mystery to his wife. In "Grief" Dominic does not understand his mother's last wish for no public display of sorrow, but he honors her request. What he learns after her death is that true grief is a private emotion, captured only in the tender memories of his mother's awareness of the smallest form of nature as the most extraordinary part of life. His grief isolates him from the public world, but it unveils a world of feeling and sensitivity hitherto unknown to him.

"The Inspector's Wife" and "The Nun's Mother" are studies of women attempting to resolve inner conflicts. At first, the inspector's

wife struggles with her interest in social distinctions and her
jealousy of the upper class, until she can reason that her marriage is
worth more than wealth and prestige. Her rationalization collapses,
however, when she learns from her husband that the daughter of a
rich family will have a happy marriage and all the other advantages
as well. In "The Nun's Mother," Maud Lattimer tries to understand
what she feels is her daughter's unnatural decision to become a nun.
The narrative carefully follows Maud's thoughts as she tries to
reconcile the physical and emotional intimacy she has known in
marriage with her daughter's calling. While recognizing that
women have "a curious streak of chastity in them, no matter how
long they were married, or how ardently they loved" (p. 196), she
still holds to the truth of her vision of her daughter's birth beginning the flow of future generations. The conflict between emotional
and spiritual truths is developed but never resolved in this highly
impressionistic story.

"The Young Girls," a story resembling Katherine Mansfield's
"Her First Ball," observes the perceptual and temperamental
differences between four girls attending a graduation party. Each
girl acts out her emotional adventure between the clashing worlds
of youth and approaching adulthood: "As they stood there, at the
window, it seemed that youth was a brightly lighted place, like the
room in which they stood; fragrant, simple, and pleasant, but that
life was dark as the dark world outside, wilful as the strong river,
and as fierce, relentless and unknowable as the night fowl that
screamed in his secretive place among the reeds" (p. 177). For Emi-
ly, the graduation party is a whirling, intoxicating initiation into
life. What happens to Dolly, however, shows that life also has its
dark and sinister side. In "A Wet Day," the final story in *The Long
Ago*, Mary Lavin returns to the storytelling patterns of her fables.
Narrated by an agnostic student, this story within a story exposes
the cruel insensitivity of Father Gogarty. He actually causes the
death of his niece's fiancé because he fears for his own health.
When he learns that the man has double pneumonia, he insists that
he leave the priest's house. The tale may appear to be a criticism of
the Roman Catholic Church, but this priest is too much of a
monster in his own right to be a symbol of religious oppression in
Ireland.

"A Cup of Tea" and "Sunday Brings Sunday," two of the most
successful stories in *The Long Ago*, resemble "Miss Holland" in
theme and technique. The plot of "A Cup of Tea" is deceptively

simple. When Sophy returns home after a three-month stay at the university, she becomes involved in an explosive argument with her mother over some boiled milk. Sophy's loss of temper and her mother's equally violent reaction seem out of proportion to the actual event. Yet the surface insignificance of "A Cup of Tea" belies the strong emotional undercurrent that exists between mother and daughter. Mary Lavin's strategy of limiting much of the third-person narrative to the perceptions of Sophy's mother is well conceived. Because Sophy's homecoming is a happy event, her mother desperately tries to keep her own emotional problems under the surface. Her happiness, however, is tainted by her excessive need for her daughter's love and approval. She seeks the natural intimacy of the mother-daughter relationship to compensate for the unfulfilled dreams of her own youth and the absence of any real intimacy with her husband. What makes her situation even more desperate is her secret knowledge that her daughter is closer emotionally to her husband than to herself.

Gradually, the emotional problems in Sophy's family emerge in spite of the sincere efforts of Sophy and her mother to avoid a crisis. Through instinctive reactions and unguarded comments, the tension increases until finally a disagreement over whether or not boiled milk spoils the taste of tea takes on tragic proportions. The truth of the situation, however, has little to do with a cup of tea. Sophy's reaction to the boiled milk is an emotional outlet for her because she feels an irritability rather than genuine pity for her mother's loneliness. The mother's anger releases her feeling that she has been betrayed by the daughter, who should have been a natural ally against her husband. When she is finally alone, Sophy, after contemplating a photograph of a young man she may someday marry, reaches out for a simple solution to her family's problems and a way of avoiding the emotional mistakes of her mother and father. Her conclusion, based more on hope and innocence than knowledge and experience, is one that a youthful Mary Lavin could have wished for as a resolution of her own family situation: "People would all have to become alike. They would have to look alike and speak alike and feel and talk and think alike. It was so simple. It was so clear! She was surprised that no one had thought of it before" (p. 37).

The complaint that nothing ever happens in Mary Lavin's stories is certainly not applicable to "Sunday Brings Sunday." Mona Clane suffers the fate of all young heroines of fiction unprepared for the wicked ways of the world. She can hardly wait for the moment

when a village lad will say "how' you" and "go walking" with her.
When her time comes, however, she finds the experience falls far
short of her romantic expectations. Unfortunately, it also introduces
her to a world of fear and suffering she never knew possible. Mona's
awkward and stumbling relationship with Jimmy Carney and her
seemingly inevitable pregnancy are the familar stuff of melodramas.
Mary Lavin's treatment of the subject, however, raises her story to a
more complex and objective level than the typical melodrama. By
narrating "Sunday Brings Sunday" through different levels of
perception and by relying upon one strong symbol as the focal point
for the reversal in Mona's fortunes, she reveals the underlying
causes of Mona's fall. This method of using several angles of vision
which eventually merge into the consciousness of the central
character resembles the points of view developed by Henry James
and Virginia Woolf. The curate's sermon at the beginning of "Sunday Brings Sunday" imposes the view of an insensitive, weary
Church upon the life of the village. His insistence on prayer as an
efficacious thing has little to do with the hard realities of his
parishioners. It also belies the fate awaiting Mona, who prays for
the day she will be courted. The view of Mona's mother represents
the attitude of the family. This perspective is also twisted, however,
because the mother's main interest in her daughter is making certain that her goodness makes her more biddable for the service. In
the process, she fails to see or understand Mona's vulnerability. The
doctor's wife is well aware of the physical dangers awaiting an innocent girl at night on a lonely country road, but she never alerts
Mona to the moral and emotional dangers of walking at night with
a country lad. The village itself condones courting as a natural and
joyful event, while never mentioning to a Mona or Jimmy the terrible consequences of their playful actions if they go too far. Each
perspective, rather than offering Mona the advantages of experience and understanding, confuses her with the narrow and
dangerous myths of the Church, family, and community.
    Mona's own view of life is symbolized by the strange words
chanted by Mad Mary, a half-crazed hag who lingers around the
churchyard each Sunday. Before she comes of age, Mona interprets
Mad Mary's strange prophecy that "Sunday brings Sunday" as
proof that the fulfillment of her dreams will be as inevitable as the
passage of time itself: "She wanted the Sundays to come on faster
and faster. She wanted the time to pass" (p. 121). After her unfortunate courtship, the saying becomes an admonition to Mona, who

does not even know that her sickness at Mass is caused by her pregnancy. Now time becomes the unrelenting bearer of the tragic consequences of life: "The year was a hobbled old hag! It was climbing over the pews. It was on top of her! It was skipping the Mondays and skipping the Thursdays and hopping from Sunday to Sunday" (p. 141). The highly impressionistic ending of "Sunday Brings Sunday" fuses all perspectives into Mona's emotional state. Her fall from grace is the fault of the Church, family, and community, but her suffering is personal and tragic. Though the village unknowingly bears the moral responsibility for Mona's fall, only Mona bears the emotional pain and the loss of hope that marks her initiation into the life of the community.

III   The Becker Wives and Other Stories

Two of the stories in *The Becker Wives* reflect a new interest in Mary Lavin's fiction. "The Becker Wives" and "A Happy Death" are closer in narrative length to the novella than the short story. In her conversations about the type of fiction which falls somewhere between the short story and the novel, Mary Lavin has made a distinction between the short novel and the novella. While defining the short novel as something squeezed together, she sees the novella as just the right length. "The Becker Wives," according to these definitions, is a squeezed-together novel. Mary Lavin had already written and published her first novel, *The House in Clewe Street*, before the publication of *The Becker Wives* in 1946. The novel, serialized in the *Atlantic Monthly* in 1944 - 45 with the early title of *Gabriel Galloway*, was published as a book in 1945. "The Becker Wives" has the same basic design as *The House in Clewe Street*. The narrative begins with an ironic view of the Beckers, a prosperous merchant family, whose most distinguished characteristic is its incredible mediocrity. The narrative voice, assuming the role of the comic stoic, establishes the same viewpoint and identical atmosphere Mary Lavin admired in Jane Austen's novels and used in her own first novel.

The opening pages of "The Becker Wives" skillfully unfold the testimony of the Becker family's mediocrity, the unerring talent of the males for selecting wives who all have the same tendency to lapse into the oblivion of a childbearing domesticity. When Theobald Becker, the youngest member of the family, defies tradition by bringing a woman of charm and imagination into the family

circle, the story changes in tone and intensity. The shift from the
comic to the tragic view in "The Becker Wives" resembles the
change that takes place in *The House in Clewe Street* when Gabriel
Galloway decides to leave home for the great city. The increased intensity in "The Becker Wives," however, is more characteristic of
Mary Lavin's short stories. Once the fantastically gifted Flora
becomes the focal point of the story, the pace of "The Becker
Wives" quickens dramatically. The narrative focuses on her delicate
consciousness until her amazing gift for mimicry finally reveals
itself as a symptom of madness. Structurally, Flora's mad confession
ends a story resembling the novel in plot and characterization but
the short story in intensity and swift insight into human emotions. A
"squeezed-together novel," with no clear identity of its own, "The
Becker Wives," nonetheless, concludes with a troubling vision of
the artist who goes too far. In the process of becoming the personalities of those around her, Flora loses her own mind and soul.
By shifting from the broad perspective of the novel to the intense
medium of the short story, "The Becker Wives" reveals the tragedy
of a young woman whose gift of insight becomes a maddening
curse, preventing her from entering the comfortable, commonsense
Becker world. Even the mediocre Beckers are aware of the magic of
what they have witnessed and the inaccessibility of that world to
them: "Their brief journey into another world had been rudely cut
short. They had merely glimpsed its strange and exciting vistas as
from afar. They had established no foothold in that far place. And
the bright enchanting creature that had opened those vistas to them
had been but a flitting spirit never meant to mix with the likes of
them."[11]
    "A Happy Death" is the same length as "The Becker Wives," but
it is entirely different in conception and method. While the
narrative remains consistent throughout the story, the emotional intensity moves the characters toward an inevitable and fitting
climax. Rather than resembling the novel, "A Happy Death" has
the same basic characteristics as Mary Lavin's short fiction, naturally extending the strategy of her short stories and exploring the same
basic theme. The story of the tragic marriage of Robert and Ella, by
Mary Lavin's own definition, is a novella rather than a short novel.
With its balance of form and content, theme and technique, "A
Happy Death" achieves the goal of being just the right length. It
richly deserves Zack Bowen's judgment as "perhaps the best of all
the Lavin stories."[12]

Before shifting to the narrative perspective of Ella, "A Happy Death" establishes the failure of her marriage through the emotional burden it places upon Nonny, the youngest of her three daughters. As Nonny struggles to attract her mother's attention to her father's coughing and moaning, she unwittingly draws out the bitter hostility Ella feels toward her husband. The daughter of a successful shopkeeper, she believes the failure of her marriage is a direct result of her husband's spineless character. Because she feels that she was trapped by his weakness into keeping a lodging house, Ella blames the loss of their social respectability and the deterioration of their house on her husband: "It was an old song. The children knew it by heart. They had heard it so often they never doubted the truth of it, and before they were of an age to form a judgment, the poison of it had entered their hearts" (p. 117).

Once the narrative shifts to Ella's perspective, the background of her unhappy marriage unveils itself. Though reduced to the state of a drudge, Ella still remembers her youthful romance with Robert, how they eloped in spite of the opposition of her parents. She also remembers her pride in his interest in poetry and her love of his fine white skin. Now, however, she sees the delicacy of Robert's nature as a foreshadowing of his physical breakdown and the failure of their marriage. Ironically, Ella's failure to sustain her belief in Robert's delicate sensibility and his fragile good looks exposes her own emotional limitations. Because her initial feelings for her husband were greatly dependent upon the attractiveness of his refined appearance, she has become obsessed with his public image now that the family fortunes have declined: "It wasn't the fact that she was worn out and had lost her looks, she could have put up with that, but it hurt her sense of pride that he should have lost his good looks, and grown into such a poor shrivelled wretch of a man" (p. 124). Unable to bear the physical deterioration of her husband, Ella insists that Robert keep up his appearance in spite of his declining health and the meagerness of their livelihood. Her unwillingness to admit the shallowness of her original feelings for her husband or to recognize the terrible effect of her twisted sense of pride on her husband's health sets the stage for the tragedy of "A Happy Death."

Without any strong and lasting love to sustain her through the family's hardships, Ella places so much importance upon keeping up appearances that she sees Robert's effort to maintain some small measure of self-respect as a willful defiance of her own plans. She flings his poetry books, once symbolic of his distinctiveness, into the fire because "all his nonsense came out of them as well" (p. 127). When he loses his position in the library because of his bad cough and accepts a lesser job as a janitor, she becomes irreparably opposed to him. Once her driving obsession seizes upon the idea of Robert sitting idly about in fine clothes to give the lodging house an air of respectability, she waits impatiently for the day when his declining health will prevent him from going to work: "For the cough was her friend. It would accomplish what she had failed to do; it would force him to give up" (p. 137).

Ironically, Ella's dream of replacing the memory of the fair young man of her youth with the image of the leisurely gentleman in the new suit is defeated rather than fulfilled by Robert's bad cough. By the time her wish is granted, Robert is so ill that he is near death and needs hospital care. Out of his delirium, however, another view emerges of their courtship and marriage. What Robert remembers is how they always wanted to be alone together, how their love isolated and protected them against the harsh feelings and judgments of others. His delirious cry that he is to die in a house of strangers is balanced by his pure memory of his love for Ella and her mad and futile pursuit of money and respectability. Ella, however, unable to move beyond surfaces, fails to reach Robert's level of understanding: "But it was all so long ago. She couldn't remember. Yet surely they had been determined to make money. Wasn't that what all normal people wanted to do—to make money and rise in the world?" (pp. 153 - 54).

Denied Robert's visionary insight into the cause of their unhappiness, Ella's mad obsession with respectability drives her even as her husband lies on his deathbed. Initially, she insists that Robert have everything that other patients in the hospital have so that the nurses will think that he is a man of importance. She worries about the class of people in his ward, and makes sure that he has a respectable supply of fruit and papers, even though he is incapable of touching either. Only when a nun gently reproves her for the waste and mentions the importance of the grace of a happy death does she stop her senseless purchases. The nun's suggestion, however, drives her to a new level of frenzied activity. The idea of a happy death now possesses her. The small mountain of decaying grapes and crumpled magazines is quickly replaced by an accumulation of crucifixes, blessed candles, and religious medals. When another patient makes a deathbed conversion, Ella is absolutely convinced that nothing in this world matters as long as her husband is granted the grace of a happy death.

When Robert briefly recovers consciousness, he receives his happy death; but the irony of the gift is that it does not come from the last sacrament of the Church. He gains a final and pure vision of Ella's former loveliness from his own heart, confessing that his only secret sin has been turning to her as the source of his happiness: " 'There's nothing to be sorry about. You always made me happy, just by being near me. Just to look at you made my heart brighter. Always. Always. It was always like that' " (p. 181). Ella's fate is to suffer the mistaken belief that Robert was denied the grace of a happy death. She fails to recognize his final bliss because she lacks his capacity for love. The agony of her final confusion and self-damnation is a fitting end for an individual whose demands for respectability on earth and in heaven have supplanted the simple hopes and needs of the human heart: "And as she was led out of the ward a few minutes later, she was still screaming and sobbing, and it was utterly incomprehensible to her that God had not heard her prayers, and had not vouchsafed to her husband the grace of a happy death" (p. 183).

The climax of "A Happy Death" once again stresses Mary Lavin's basic theme that individuals of radically different interests and sensibilities rarely achieve even a simple, momentary understanding of each other's needs. From the bitter fate of Manny and Annie Ryan to the tragic ordeal of Robert and Ella, the best hopes for happiness are crushed by the failure of the individual to rise above his own narrow desires and understand the emotional needs of another human being. In "A Happy Death," Robert's vision the moment before his death creates a sense of emotional triumph that rarely appears in Mary Lavin's early fiction. It does, however, suggest a philosophy that later sustained her through her own tragedies. There is much misunderstanding and loneliness in the Lavin canon, but as death becomes more and more of a reality in her later fiction, Robert's discovery that happiness coexists with great suffering assumes more and more importance until it becomes the stated philosophy of her most autobiographical character.

CHAPTER 3

The Novels: The Irish Middle Class and the Irish Mother

I N her preface to *Selected Stories,* Mary Lavin states
her dissatisfaction with her two long novels. In spite of her early
interest in the novel form, she wishes that she "could break up" the
ones she has written "into the few short stories they ought to have
been in the first place."[1] Lacking selectivity, her novels fall short of
revealing the truth. Only her short fiction takes its "shape as well as
matter" from "the writer's own character."[2]

In her unpublished notes for an essay on the short story, she also
acknowledges her preference for the short story.[3] She believes the
novel requires a full knowledge of history or a commitment to
endless hours of research to recapture the historical experience. The
short story, however, does not depend upon the writer's memory of
facts or his avid interest in history. Its brevity and intensity are best
suited for capturing the immediacy of impressions. Admitting her
own difficulties with the novel form, Mary Lavin considers the
problem of stamina, but recalls that she wrote her two long novels
with a great deal of care and concentration. Rather than a shrinking
from the rigors of novel writing, her own decision to write short
stories was based upon an awareness of the needs and limitations of
her own nature. She sees this recognition of one's limitations,
strengths, and the particular blend of both, as a major step in the
writer's development of his craft.

I   *"Jane Austen and the Construction of the Novel"*

Whatever Mary Lavin has since learned about her own strengths
and weaknesses, she began her career with a solid understanding of
the history of the novel. In 1936, two years before the appearance of
her first published short story, she completed a thesis on Jane
44

Austen for her Master of Arts degree at University College, Dublin. "Jane Austen and the Construction of the Novel" shows a wide-ranging knowledge of the great novelists and a deep interest in the structure of their novels. The thesis includes detailed observations on the English novelists from Richardson, Fielding, and Austen to Dickens, Thackeray, Hardy, and Woolf. It also makes observations on Tolstoy, Mann, and Hemingway. What she seeks in the novels of the great writers is support for a set of abstract rules for the construction of a good novel. These rules, derived from the Aristotelian theory of the epic, establish the natural divisions of a good story as plot, character, sentiment, diction, and decoration. For the novelist to achieve excellence, he needs to fulfill certain requirements inherent in each division of the novel.

The first part of Mary Lavin's thesis, her discussion of the requirements of the good novel, offers several insights into the strategy of her own novels, *The House in Clewe Street* and *Mary O'Grady*. In her comments on plot, she stresses the importance of a strong narrative based on a logical probability of events. She also believes that the novelist should take advantage of plot agents, dramatic irony, proper magnitude of events, and the omniscient point of view to make events more adhesive and credible. Character, she says, should be inseparable from plot. It should also establish an affinity and universality with the reader. The chief purpose of plot and character is to reveal the significant influences which shape human destiny. Mary Lavin defines sentiment as the moral of the work, and believes most books have a definite moral purpose. Recognizing the dangers of a laid-on morality, however, she argues that the best method of the novelist is to make his views part of the texture of the story. The novelist needs to remember that ominiscience is a privilege rather than a weapon. Diction, the style of the novel, and decoration, the description of character and scenery, should be characterized by clarity and suitability. Borrowing once again from Aristotle, she defines style as perspicacious without being mean. Dialogue, she believes, is most effective when it follows the rule of realism.

Mary Lavin's discussion of Jane Austen in the second part of her thesis also reveals attitudes and judgments that shaped her own novels. She sees Jane Austen as an intellectual rather than emotional writer, more French than English in her approach to the novel. *Pride and Prejudice* is as nearly perfect as any novel in English literature because of its well-constructed plot and its realistic characterizations. What she admires particularly in *Pride and Prejudice* is the way in which the opening combines incident and introductory materials. Too many novelists fail because they open their works with a long and boring third-person exposition of past history. She also believes that Jane Austen was the first English novelist to appreciate the beauty of proper magnitude, the balance between subject and form, and to understand the need for developing the complexity of her characters for the sake of realism while still gaining universal interest and approval by the merest suggestion of type. Being an intellectual rather than emotional writer, Jane Austen's vision of life, the sentiment in her novels, is comic rather than tragic. Using as her standard Walpole's view that life is a comedy to the thinking man and a tragedy to the man who feels, Mary Lavin sees Jane Austen as a happy stoic who stressed taste, common sense, and reasonable conformity. Always implicitly rather than explicitly stated, Jane Austen's moral view reflects a coldness and disinterestedness which make her intensely modern in outlook.

II   The House in Clewe Street

Mary Lavin's first novel, *The House in Clewe Street*, utilizes several of the judgments made in her thesis. The novel is divided into three parts and the title of each part bears the name of a character who figures prominently in the major events of the novel. In this way she achieves in the very outline of the novel the sense that plot and character are inseparable. She also hints that the purpose of each major part of the novel is the revelation of some stage in the destinies of her chief characters. The title of the first part of the novel, "Theodore and Cornelius," anticipates the idea of inheritance which dominates the early episodes. Theodore Coniffe, the family patriarch and the leading property owner in Castlerampart, is the grandfather of Gabriel Galloway, the novel's young hero. Cornelius Galloway, the husband of Theodore's youngest daughter, is Gabriel's father. "Gabriel Galloway," the original title of *The House in Clewe Street*, is the title of the second part of the novel. It bears the name of the novel's hero and traces his early life after the deaths of his father and grandfather. Together, the two sections make up the first half of the novel, which ends just as Gabriel makes his first tentative steps toward freedom and young adulthood. Gabriel's tragic involvement with Onny Soraghan, the family servant, is the focal point of the last half of the novel.

"Gabriel and Onny" traces the emotional and moral mistakes Gabriel makes under the influence of his intimate relationship with Onny and his friendship with Sylvester. His acceptance of his own responsibility for Onny's tragic death is the beginning of his initiation into adulthood.

Mary Lavin opens *The House in Clewe Street* with a strategy she discovered in Jane Austen's novels. In her thesis she complains that the opening of the English novel is traditionally dull because it is weighted down with a summary of the past events needed by the reader to understand the current developments in the novel. Jane Austen's way of avoiding this tedium was to work her background material into the texture of the opening scene. In *The House in Clewe Street*, Mary Lavin tries for the same effect by beginning the narrative as Theodore Coniffe waits for the return of Cornelius Galloway and his youngest daughter from their honeymoon. While Theodore is waiting for the return of the "Happy Pair," he engages in several brief conversations which establish his character and social standing in the community. Physically trim and mentally alert despite his seventy years, Theodore is dressed as a man who has made his living through cleverness rather than physical labor. When Colonel Fanshawe rides up, however, the narrative quickly establishes the social and cultural differences between the two men. By pointing out the differences in their clothes—the colonel dresses gracefully, Theodore respectably—and by drawing attention to Theodore's hidden contempt for the colonel's haughty bay mare, the narrator makes it obvious that Theodore feels socially inferior to his aristocratic neighbor in spite of his own prosperity. This brief meeting between the two men also sketches social attitudes that are to play a major role in the approaching tragedy of the Happy Pair. Even the horse ridden by Colonel Fanshawe foreshadows the tragedy. Finally, this opening conversation, coupled with the narrator's description of the social climate of Castlerampart, establishes the novel's chief interest as social manners and the moral conduct of its characters.

The social and moral standard by which the narrator observes and judges the characters and events in *The House in Clewe Street* is closely associated with the life-style of Theodore Coniffe. Conservative, Catholic, and solidly middle class, he stands between the two extremes of wealth and poverty associated with the Big House and the post-Great Famine poverty. The principal property holder in Castlerampart, Theodore is still uncomfortable and insecure in the presence of Colonel Fanshawe. Yet he is repulsed by the poverty-stricken huts isolated from the town by the river and the ancient rampart. Theodore's chief characteristic is his obsession with his property. Brief conversations with two of his tenants expose his concern for the condition of his houses, which he values far more than the human life within them: " 'Ah, yes, a house is a delicate article. A house is ten times more delicate than the people that live in it. That is a strange thing, isn't it? But it's true. A person may suffer a bruise or a break, but the bone will knit and the skin will heal. That is not the way with a house.' "[4]

Theodore Coniffe's materialism is so ludicrous it acts as a comic foil for the more moderate narrative view. Nevertheless the narrator's voice echoes the social and moral standards of the Irish middle-class world of Castlerampart. Extreme views, some naive, others insensitive and ignorant, appear in *The House in Clewe Street*, but the general perspective of Mary Lavin's novel reflects the values she observed when she lived with her mother's relatives in Athenry. As Gabriel Galloway grows up, he rebels against his middle-class environment; but when he falls into great difficulties in the city, he is judged and judges himself by Castlerampart's standards. Thus the novel's solidity is in its consistent moral and social tone. Its limitations, however, are also to be found in its conventional point of view.

Once the novel's perspective is established, the narrative turns to the business of providing the background leading up to the expected arrival of the Happy Pair. The catalyst for this backward movement is the narrator's inside information that "the wedding of Lily Coniffe to Cornelius Galloway was a source of bitter mortification to her sisters, Theresa and Sara, but particularly to Theresa" (pp. 17 - 18). The justification for this review of past events, a tedious practice in the English novel, is that the story behind Theresa's bitterness is well known in the community. Thus the narrator, reflecting the collective consciousness of Castlerampart, assumes the role of town chronicler to tell the story which everyone in the novel already knows either through memory or gossip.

The story within a novel begins with a brief summary of the early family years of Theodore and Katherine Coniffe, and Theodore's doting affection for his two daughters, Theresa and Sara. When Theresa is fifteen and Sara thirteen, however, the family's complacency is shaken by the news of Katherine's pregnancy. The expected arrival immediately assumes mock-epic importance in the town, while casting a tragicomic atmosphere over the family. Theodore is overjoyed at the news because he sincerely believes fate would not intervene this way unless it intended finally to give him a son. Katherine, however, is more sensitive to social realities than cosmic forces. Knowing her neighbors, she accurately predicts the news of her pregnancy will make the elderly couple the laughingstock of Castlerampart. The townspeople go Katherine one better, however, by fitting Theodore's fatalistic vision to their own comic view of her pregnancy. What they anticipate is that fate will give the Coniffes another daughter rather than their first son. Unfortunately, what happens shocks even the most skeptical of the townspeople.

Katherine's death in childbirth briefly raises the level of the narrative to tragedy. The irony of the birth of the Coniffe's third daughter is lost in the unexpected sorrow of Theodore and his girls. Instead of turning to the emotional needs of his older daughters, however, Theodore, in his moment of grief, gives them the responsibility for the new child. Not only do Theresa and Sara have to endure the tragic loss of their mother, they have to turn away from their own adolescent dreams and accept the adult responsibility of caring for their sister. The emotional consequences of Theodore's decision finally materialize when Lily becomes sixteen. When Theodore is forced to recognize that Lily is approaching the age of womanhood and marriage, he remembers his old responsibilities to Theresa and Sara. At this critical moment, while Theodore is discovering that he has made potential spinsters out of his daughters, the narrative conveniently drops Cornelius Galloway into the plot as the eligible bachelor Theodore so desperately needs to marry off either Theresa or Sara.

The arrival in Castlerampart of the new solicitor from Dublin just at the moment Theodore Coniffe decides that he must find a husband for one of his daughters is a blatant example of the strategy of coincidence which plagues the English novel from *Pamela* to *Tess of the d'Urbervilles*. Unfortunately, coincidence plays a major role in the entire narrative structure of *The House in Clewe Street*. Its first appearance in the novel draws to the surface the emotional problems that have been developing in the Coniffe family ever since Katherine's death. Theodore's decision to marry Cornelius to one of his daughters serves only to magnify the limitations of Theresa and Sara. Theresa's self-discipline becomes strident in the presence of Cornelius, while Sara's timidity appears as little more than a thin disguise for her foolishness. Fortunately, Cornelius not only knows what is behind Theodore's interest in his career, he secretly approves of it. His only problem is deciding which of the Coniffe sisters would make the better wife.

Fate intervenes once again in *The House in Clewe Street* in the form of Lily. When Cornelius sees her sitting in the garden, he suddenly recognizes her youthful beauty. Realizing that his indecisiveness has prepared him for this moment of love, he refuses to ignore what chance has shown him. The next stage in the history of the Coniffe family begins when Cornelius accepts his fate by proposing marriage to the youngest Coniffe daughter:

> He went along the passage and put his hand on the handle of the door, calm, resolute, well aware of the hurt and injustice of his actions, and of the pain and disappointment that he had caused, but fortified, upheld, exalted by the feeling that a force greater than himself had swept down upon him, and imposed its own will upon his sightless designs. He had been ready to make sacrifices for the sake of his ambitions. As a reward it had been revealed to him in a single moment that there were no sacrifices to make. (pp. 68 - 69)

Galloway's proposal to Lily appears to be the beginning of great happiness; in reality, however, it contains the seeds of tragedy. After briefly describing the strain in the family caused by the unexpected turn of events, the narrative returns to the present scene. Once the Happy Pair return from their honeymoon, the conditions which cause the tragedy are unknowingly imposed upon the family by Cornelius. Deciding that Theodore knows how to make money but not how to spend it, he convinces his father-in-law that the Coniffes should enjoy the pleasures and refinements of wealth as much as the Fanshawes. Unfortunately, Cornelius's desire to buy his way into tradition proves his undoing. His tragic flaw, his defiance of social customs, is the perfect one in a novel of manners. The narrator, after Cornelius's death, stresses the difference between the servile tradition, represented by the Coniffes in spite of their wealth, and the aristocratic tradition, represented by the Fanshawes. The very nature of Cornelius's death underlines the folly of his efforts to defy social differences. Theodore's brief meeting with Colonel Fanshawe takes on its full symbolic significance when Cornelius is thrown by Willful Filly and killed when the horse falls upon him. The accident occurs during a foxhunt led by the Master of the Hunt, Colonel Fanshawe. His only comment on Cornelius's death is a fitting epitaph for this young social rebel: " 'You have to be bred to hunting' " (p. 90).

The narration of events leading up to the second tragedy in the Coniffe family also contains faint foreshadowings of future crises. Cornelius's rejection of Theresa and Sara has the effect of permanently fixing the extremes of their personalities. While Theresa becomes even more domineering in family affairs, Sara retreats even more into her timidity. Lily's pleas to the contrary, her older sisters, particularly Theresa, feel betrayed by the marriage. Her only protection against Theresa's wrath is her position in the family as Cornelius's wife. Also a factor in the future affairs of the family is the compensation Theresa and Sara draw from their religion for being spinsters. The limitations of Theresa and Sara become virtues in the eyes of the congregation. Sternness and timidity are seen by the public eye as strict discipline and self-sacrifice. The end result is that Theresa and Sara, denied prominence in the community through marriage, assume social importance and influence through their religious activities. Thus the strict observance of religious duties becomes an inextricable part of the Coniffe's social life. Finally, the narrative voice itself hints at the future course of the novel in its summary of the tragic career of Cornelius Galloway. Though Cornelius failed, his fault, according to the narrator, was not a lack of courage or determination. Only by falling short of his ambition had he lost credit for his sound qualities in the eyes of the community and his in-laws. On the other hand, there are young men who do not have Cornelius's strengths, though they share his ambition:

Many young men may have felt themselves in the same position as Cornelius, in fact cities are full of such young men, who feel that they were born for better things, but to most of them this is only a cause of hopeless despair and bitterness. They throw themselves into some literary or artistic movement, where they can eventually persuade themselves that their poverty is Revolt, and that their squalor is Reality. (p. 100)

The narrator's derogatory remarks about literary movements that reinforced the young artist's alienation from society have no immediate bearing upon the events of *The House in Clewe Street*. Not until Cornelius's son, Gabriel, approaches young manhood does the judgment set down at the conclusion of the first part of the novel take on major importance. The authorial comments do, however, reinforce the major thematic and structural concepts of the novel.

Clearly implied is the narrator's preference for behavior that reflects
social conventions rather than defies them. What follows in *The
House in Clewe Street* is the story of Gabriel Galloway, who will be
judged by Castlerampart's standards. The narrative view tends to
be sympathetic toward Gabriel, particularly since he inherits the
difficult emotional climate growing out of the tragic deaths of his
grandmother and father. Always in the background, however, are
the established norms of the middle class.

The narrative of "Gabriel Galloway" opens when the young hero
of *The House in Clewe Street* is six years old. The particular day is
significant both in the life of Gabriel and in the Coniffe family
history. For Gabriel, this is the first day he puts on his own trousers.
His triumph, however, clashes sharply with the mood of the
household. The reason Gabriel has been left to himself is that the
family's normal routine has been disrupted by the death of
Theodore Coniffe. Thus the early history of Gabriel Galloway
begins with the death of the family patriarch. The further
significance of this day is that it marks the beginning of Gabriel's
perceptual history. A great deal of narrative attention is given to the
way in which "leaf by leaf, petal by petal, our impressions are laid
down" (p. 142). Ironically, the family prevents Gabriel from receiving any physical impressions of his grandfather's death. Instead,
they send him for the day to the Soraghans, a poor family that
provides a continual flow of servant girls for the respectable middle-
class families of Castlerampart. Denied any contact with death,
Gabriel is suddenly confronted with another new world of impressions and his first meeting with the girl who will play a major
role in his later social and moral history.

Gabriel's visit to the Soraghans is his initial adventure beyond the
security of his home. What he encounters for the first time is the
great social difference between the Coniffes and the Soraghans, a
difference that goes beyond economics. In a perceptible shift in
sympathy, the narrator points out how the real secret of class tyranny is not so much money as it is the loud and demanding voice of
presumed authority. As for poor Ireland, this tyranny of the loud
voices over the thin voices is "the politician over the electorate, the
priest over the sinner, the husband over the wife, the teacher over
the child. It was even the tyranny of tinker over tinker; the real
tyranny of Ireland, where, by a loud voice, all things are gained" (p.
129).

Gabriel is far too young to understand the full social and moral implications of his visit to the Soraghans. The narrator, however, firmly establishes the novel's social theme as the standard by which Gabriel's future actions are to be judged. Throughout his early and adolescent years, he will have to face this tyranny of the loud voices in the figure of the domineering Aunt Theresa. Her only claim to authority is her own sense of self-righteousness and her talent for manipulating the weak and the timid. What Gabriel will need to overcome his aunt's tyranny, he first discovers at the Soraghans. The Soraghan children's natural independence completely surprises him. In contrast to his own submissive life, he encounters the brash behavior of the youngest girl, Onny. Gabriel finds her sitting naked behind a hedge, completely oblivious to her family's efforts to find her. Not only does this moment foreshadow Gabriel's later involvement with Onny and his heroic rescue of her from the flooded river, it creates in Gabriel's soul the first stirrings of independence.

Ironically, in spite of the fact that Theodore Coniffe's death establishes Theresa as the uncrowned queen of the household, the bizarre events of the funeral, which include an outrageously comic race to the cemetery between the funeral parties, force Gabriel to take another step away from the oppressive atmosphere of his home. Enraged by the antics of the funeral party, the local priest, acting out the tyranny of the loud voice over the weak voice, turns his attention to the youngest and smallest Coniffe. He takes out his frustrations on poor Gabriel by ordering him to school so that he can receive a proper religious training. The priest's words are a slap in the face for Theresa and Sara because of their activities in the Church. For Gabriel, however, they announce the beginning of another new experience.

One event associated with his grandfather's death places Gabriel under closer scrutiny than ever before. Much to Theresa's shock and disappointment, Theodore's will leaves the entire property to his grandson. Theresa relaxes, however, when she learns that Gabriel is not to gain actual control of the property until he is twenty-five years old. Knowing that she has full control over family affairs for many years to come, she becomes even more determined to impose her authority upon the child. Theodore's will in itself is a tribute to the brief interlude of the Happy Pair, but the age stipulation is a reminder of Cornelius's reckless character and the possibility that it has been inherited by his son. It is this side of Gabriel's character, whether real or imagined, that Theresa holds over the child. Her strictness, however, is as much a measure of revenge for past disap-

pointments as it is a way of making sure that the sins of the father
are not those of the son.

One of Gabriel's first discoveries in school is that he is a better
scholar than his fellow classmates. Of more importance, however, is
his realization that social distinctions exist between town and country students. Once again, the culprit is social convention. The
original custom was for a child to bring a sod of turf each day for
the school fire. When it became too difficult for the town children
to find turf, they were allowed to bring a half-penny as a substitute.
Eventually the difference between contributions took on a social
value, with the copper piece assuming a certain dignity in contrast
with the sod of flaky turf. This distinction was made even more
definite by the deliberate arrangement of the town boys on one
side of the aisle and those from the country on the other. The
difference in dress between the town boys in their ready-made suits
and country lads in their rough tweed suits adds one final twist to
the pattern of social discrimination developed out of the simple
tradition of bringing a sod of turf for the school fire.

In spite of the social line drawn between town and country,
Gabriel responds warmly to Larry Soraghan's offer of friendship.
His decision is hardly a conscious act of rebellion against the
system, but it is a favorable indication of character. Obviously
Gabriel's desire to become friends with Larry is unacceptable to
Theresa Coniffe. And since Gabriel has not yet learned to act in-
dependently, he surrenders to his aunt's will. A natural leader in the
classroom, he becomes an outsider, a figure of ridicule, in the
playground. Ironically, Theresa's own desire to find a proper
playmate for Gabriel leads to a much more dangerous friendship
than any with a boy from the lower classes. Whatever social benefit
the arranged meeting with Sylvester, the son of a respectable widow
of a Dublin artist, is supposed to have upon Gabriel, their developing relationship stirs an even greater sense of independence in
Gabriel's soul. Sylvester's bold self-assurance so deeply affects
Gabriel that he sees all his other interests and companionships as
trivial.

Shortly after his first meeting with Sylvester, Gabriel undergoes
his first spiritual crisis. Resentful that he has to attend church on a
Holy Day, he contemplates the previously unthinkable sin of missing Mass. When Larry Soraghan turns up at the very moment of
Gabriel's restlessness, the two decide to risk God's anger by having
an adventure instead of attending Mass. Far more imaginary than

real, the outcome of their adventure, nevertheless, is as terrifying and threatening as the meeting with the strange man in Joyce's "An Encounter." For Gabriel and Larry, the decision to buy oranges with the collection-plate money leads to their undoing. Already stricken by guilt, they are shaken by the red freckles in the oranges. Not realizing that the red splashes are tiny pockets of rich juice, they assume that they are drops of blood—God's blood.

Torn between believing and disbelieving that God has sent a sign of his displeasure, Gabriel turns to the more experienced Sylvester to resolve the problem. Unfortunately, Sylvester's decision that Gabriel miss Mass again to see if God sends another sign, leads to a real disaster. This time Gabriel has to face the terrible wrath of his Aunt Theresa. Caught in the act of missing Mass, he learns there are more immediate things to fear than the ways of God to man. For the first time in his life, he sees an open display of Theresa's bitterness toward him. Too young to know the reason for her antagonism, Gabriel does learn that it is to his advantage not to give Theresa any further opportunities to show her feelings. Though Theresa decides that she will not expose Gabriel's sinfulness to public view because of the social embarrassment to the family, she becomes even more determined to watch her nephew for any further manifestations of the reckless behavior of his father.

The rest of Gabriel's youth is spent within the tense, oppressive atmosphere created by Aunt Theresa. One direct result of Theresa's watchfulness is the family's decision not to send Gabriel to boarding school. Ostensibly, the reason for keeping Gabriel at home is that his social and financial position in Castlerampart is already assured because of his inheritance. But even the timid Sara knows that Theresa does not want to risk sending Gabriel to the same school system that educated Gabriel Galloway, and was chiefly "responsible for giving him such an erroneous interpretation of money and its uses that, as Theresa firmly believed, God himself had had to intervene and correct him, by removing him from the scene of his errors—with the help of Willful Filly" (p. 224).

Gabriel's fainthearted efforts to overcome his aunt's tyranny are rarely effective, but time itself works to his benefit. When he reaches the age of sixteen, the family is forced to make a decision about his future because he has completed his education at the local school. Forced by circumstances to do something with her nephew, Theresa decides that the path of least harm is to the technical school in Draghead. Gabriel's new freedom is rather insignificant,

however, when compared to Sylvester's news that he will attend art
school in Dublin. Chastised by Sylvester for giving in to the narrow
judgments of his family, Gabriel realizes he still lacks the courage
and maturity to challenge Aunt Theresa's authority. In spite of the
fact that he recognizes the truth in Sylvester's warning that
Castlerampart is closing around his neck, Gabriel cannot respond to
Sylvester's urgings that they join forces in Dublin. As the second
part of the novel closes, Gabriel knows that his life is limited by the
arbitrary authority of his Aunt Theresa, but he has not faced a crisis
severe enough to force him to act against his family's wishes.

The crisis in "Gabriel and Onny," as the title suggests, takes the
form of an emotional and sexual awakening. Thus the pattern of
The House in Clewe Street, once Gabriel enters the novel, is similar
to the form of the modern *Bildungsroman*. As in *A Portrait of the
Artist as a Young Man, The Way of All Flesh*, and *Sons and Lovers*
an oppressive family atmosphere eventually interferes with the
young hero's budding sexuality. His initial rebellion against
authority comes about through the irresistible desire for self-
identity and self-expression rather than through any conscious or
deliberately defined effort to defy the oppressiveness of family life.

The last part of *The House in Clewe Street*, which in narrative
length is as long as the first two sections combined, opens with the
death of Gabriel's mother. Though Gabriel believes that his
mother's death has brought about an incalculable change in his life,
he is completely unaware of the way in which that change is taking
shape. Whatever grief he feels has little influence on his destiny.
Ironically, it is a shift in domestic policy related to the family
tragedy that sets in motion the great change in Gabriel's life. With
her usual lack of compassion, Theresa uses her sister's death to get
rid of the family's servant, Mary Ellen. In place of Mary Ellen,
Theresa hires Onny, the youngest of the Soraghan girls, to do the
odd jobs usually performed by Mary Ellen. Thus, at the very moment Gabriel begins his classes at the technical school, the girl who
inspired the first faint stirrings of independence in Gabriel's soul
becomes an integral part of the Coniffe's domestic life.

Gabriel's rediscovery of Onny's free spirit takes place within the
same setting in which he first learned the full extent of his aunt's
antagonism toward him. He discovers that Onny shares his reluctance to attend evening Mass. His chance encounter with Onny outside the boundaries of the Coniffe household has a profound effect
upon Gabriel. By seeing the difference between Onny's servility

with his aunts and her independence once free of her domestic chores, Gabriel begins to understand some of the social and economic restrictions imposed upon the laboring class. More significantly, while the contrast in Onny's behavior raises Gabriel's social consciousness a few degrees, the brief personal encounter between the two sharpens his perception of Onny as an attractive, energetic young woman with a fine figure under her shabby dress.

Moved by social sympathy and sexual attraction, Gabriel lacks only the opportunity to become emotionally involved with Onny. The moment comes in an almost Hardyesque situation and setting. While wandering restlessly along the edge of the river, Gabriel accidentally encounters Onny. Dressed for an evening of gaiety with the young people of Castlerampart, she seems a vision of all the simple joys and pleasures of life denied to him by his aunt's tyranny. In a scene that has both present and future narrative significance, Gabriel helps Onny to take a shortcut across the shallow river by leaping from stone to stone. The minor adventure is so exaggerated out of proportion by the emotions of the young people that by the time they reach the other shore Onny is no longer the kitchen drudge and Gabriel is no longer alone in the evenings.

Until Gabriel's secret involvement with Onny, the narrative, even with its formal voice and its unquestioning support of convention, still maintains its credibility. The elevated language does seem more appropriate to an eighteenth- or nineteenth-century novel than to a modern one, but the narrator practices a restraint in commenting on characters and events reminiscent of the strategy in Jane Austen's novels. The middle-class attitude of Castlerampart with its social and moral conventions is restrictive, but the narrator's sympathy with Gabriel's growing pains and his difficulties with Aunt Theresa create an early sense of balance and proportion in the novel. Once the novel reaches the point of Gabriel's relationship with Onny, however, the narrator begins to make judgments about Gabriel's character that are simply not supported by his past behavior.

One of the most striking departures from character occurs at the very moment Gabriel is drawn toward Onny. At first repulsed by the tastelessness of Onny's dress, Gabriel sees that her motley appearance is appropriate for the anticipated evening of gaiety. For this bit of insight Gabriel is credited by the narrator with "a depth of sensitiveness that analyzed further than most people" because

Onny's dress would have "horrified the tastes of the averagely sensitive person" (p. 290). Rather, Gabriel's behavior at the moment seems more a result of the increasing demands of adolescence than any perceptual sensitivity. The moment itself marks the beginning of an unintentional narrative conflict between the actual thoughts and actions of a timid and undistinguished young man and the narrator's insistence that this same young man has character and insight. Apart from the outdated narrative voice, Gabriel's credibility becomes the most serious problem in the novel.

Once drawn together, Gabriel and Onny decide to meet every evening after she finishes her domestic chores. By meeting Onny secretly in the ruins of an old tower associated in Gabriel's mind with childhood fantasies of freedom and adventure, Gabriel has the best of both dreamworlds of childhood and adolescence. As to the secrecy of their meetings, Gabriel readily accepts the need for great discretion because, for all his insight into the nature of things, he lacks the courage to challenge the authority of the social and moral conventions of Castlerampart and the town's chief standard bearer, Aunt Theresa. When Aunt Sara hints at a possible attraction between Gabriel and Onny, Theresa quickly points out the clear social and moral distinction any respectable individual would draw between the young people: " 'Gabriel is a gentleman!' said Theresa. 'And there can be no comparison, except in the head of a fool, between the son of a gentleman and a slut of a servant with flashy legs' " (p. 309).

It takes a near tragedy to shake Gabriel out of the grip of the town's conventions. His moment of truth comes when, for the first time since the beginning of their secret meetings, Onny fails to turn up at the ruined tower. Gabriel's initial confusion and concern quickly changes to jealousy and disgust when he mistakenly believes that Onny has gone off for a cheap joyride with some of her friends. After Gabriel learns that he is wrong, he returns to the vicinity of the tower to search for her. In one of few melodramatic sequences in Mary Lavin's fiction, Gabriel finds Onny caught in one of the boughs overhanging the swirling waters of the river. With a daring effort he crawls out onto the flooded river while clinging to the bough and brings the unconscious girl safely back to the shore. The rescue accomplished, Gabriel carries Onny to the Coniffe house, where she soon recovers from her ordeal.

Even though the near tragedy is averted, Gabriel finds that his relationship with Onny, though not exposed by the misadventure, has reached a dangerous level of involvement. At first deceived into believing that Onny threw herself into the river out of shame, he still feels, after he learns the truth, that he is at least indirectly responsible for her frightening encounter with the poacher who chased her into the river. Even her deceit convinces him that she is in need of some sort of moral guidance. Neither loving greatly nor too little, he tells Onny that he is now bound to her for life.

In spite of his pledge, Gabriel still recognizes the practical necessity for continued secrecy. As for Onny, she prefers the limitations of her situation because she simply refuses to believe the day will ever come when she is the mistress of the Coniffe household. The moment, however, is forced to a crisis again by the irrepressible Aunt Theresa. Sensing a possible attraction between Onny and her nephew, she decides to point out the social flaws of their servant. What Gabriel listens to is a cruel attack on Onny and her social class. Aunt Theresa's comments range from her firm belief that Onny lacks grace because people like the Soraghans are inferior in the blood to people like the Coniffes to her strong suspicion that Onny's personal habits are filthy because the Soraghans live more like animals than human beings. No matter what Theresa has suffered herself, her judgment of Onny exposes a lack of humanity firmly rooted in the very prosperity she enjoys as a Coniffe. She comes to represent the worse side of the Irish middle class. Unfeelingly concerned with appearances and the family's social and financial standing, she anticipates Bedelia Grimes, who destroys the emotional life of her family in order to preserve the family business. Denied love early in their lives, both women ruthlessly exploit the idea of social respectability to manipulate their families' emotions.

Theresa's vicious remarks serve only to convince Gabriel that he must do something to fulfill his pledge to Onny. His decision, aided by an increase in allowance money and a birthday present of five pounds from Sara, is to take Onny away with him to a new life in Dublin. Relying upon Sylvester for immediate lodgings, he takes his first major step into manhood. Unfortunately, his action is so shaped by a series of misadventures, misunderstandings, and mistaken feelings, it seems destined to failure. Even though the fall of the young hero once he enters the great city has sociological and mythical precedence, Gabriel's own character does much to damage the credibility of the initiation theme in *The House in Clewe Street*. What should be the most interesting episode in the novel becomes the least believable because Gabriel, in spite of his bold action, is so much a product of the Coniffe environment that he becomes insufferable when away from it.

Once aboard the train to Dublin, Gabriel begins to show the same social snobbery toward Onny that he found so detestable in his aunt. When Onny strikes up a conversation with some of the passengers, he criticizes her for being interested in common and foolish people. Reproved himself for fault-finding, he assures her that " 'to wish to correct slight imperfections in a person who is dear to me is not finding fault' " (p. 379). Whatever the rationale, the snobbish behavior continues after the young couple arrives in Dublin. Equipped with a guidebook, Gabriel tries to make their first day in Dublin a cultural experience. While he examines the buildings and monuments of the city, Onny responds naturally and warmly to its teeming life. Gabriel's reaction to Onny, however, is entirely negative. Sensing more than ever their differences in manner, vocabulary, gestures, bearing, and interest, he finds it more and more difficult to avoid the fact that her freedom from discipline is what he finds so attractive about her, and that their differences more than their emotions are what have drawn them together.

The relationship between Gabriel and Onny has the potential of balancing the extreme personalities of the young couple. Once they are settled in Sylvester's studio, however, their differences become even more pronounced. Already stiff and pompous, Gabriel feels imprisoned in the atmosphere of his own provinciality. Instead of the artist colony having a liberating effect upon Gabriel, it hardens his conventional attitude. Surprised when Onny refuses to attend Mass on their first Sunday in Dublin, Gabriel wants to make their relationship respectable by finding a job and marrying. Onny, however, has no trouble at all falling into her new life-style. Rather attractive and spontaneous, she quickly forms an intimacy with Sylvester and his artist friends that shocks Gabriel. As for her life with Gabriel, Onny is quite content with the present arrangement. Whenever Gabriel discusses their future, she accepts his plans for marriage without protest but also without any enthusiasm or encouragement.

A surprise visit by Theresa and Sara to Sylvester's studio while Gabriel is out acts as a further source of alienation for Gabriel and Onny. Gabriel is greatly disturbed by Onny's rude treatment of his aunts. Their abortive visit, however, has an even stronger effect on Gabriel, forcing him to examine his decision in terms of its full

social implications: "It was one thing to break free from the subjec-
tion of an Aunt Theresa. It was another thing to cut yourself off
from the place of your birth, the town where your mother and
father had made themselves known and respected, where before
them your grandfather. . . . Gabriel's thoughts were arrested by a
remembrance of old Theodore, and he was overcome by feelings
once more" (p. 447).

As Gabriel's sense of the value of patrimony reasserts itself, Onny
drifts more and more into Sylvester's world. Over Gabriel's protests,
she becomes the model for Telman Young, one of Sylvester's
painter friends. Unknown to Gabriel, she also becomes the lover of
Sylvester and Telman. When Gabriel tries to undo some of the
harm by carrying out his promise to marry her, he discovers that
Onny is pregnant. This melodramtic pattern reaches its climax
when Onny deserts Gabriel and decides to have an abortion. Shortly
after the operation, she is found wandering in a state of delirium by
the Dublin police—by the next morning she is dead. While all this
is taking place, Gabriel becomes less and less credible as a character.
His renewed sense of the value of his life in Castlerampart literally
drives Onny out of the studio. Even Sylvester, who usually refrains
from any hard judgments, finds Gabriel something of a fool.

Gabriel's future comes down to deciding whether or not to
become involved in the inquest into Onny's death. His first instinct
is to return to the sanctity of Castlerampart. In a rather amazing
turnabout, his oppressive childhood days now "shine with golden
innocence" (p. 529). As for Aunt Theresa, Gabriel now recognizes
the simple virtue that he (and the narrator) somehow or other missed when he was a child:

To Theresa, even more than to Sara, his mind turned in its anguish and he
yearned for her strong hand jerking him to her side more even than he
longed for Sara's soft palm on his forehead, for now in a flash he came to
the knowledge that had been denied to him in all the years, that whatever
his Aunt Theresa might think of him she would stand by him against the
world. No matter how great his guilt she would take his part against his ac-
cusers. And no matter how fierce the onslaught of his retribution, she would
stiffen herself to oppose it, and behind her dominating figure, austere and
hard, neither the importunities of the Soraghans nor the inquisitiveness of
outsiders would be of any avail. (p. 529)

Fortified by his discovery of the enduring value of his childhood
days, he decides that, as much as he would like to return home, his
real duty is to accept the responsibility for Onny's death and return

to the city. In a scene resembling the final moment in *Sons and Lovers*, Gabriel turns his back on his childhood and any possible escape from the responsibilities of adulthood. As he strides toward Dublin, he takes his first real steps toward manhood. Unfortunately, any comparison between the endings of *Sons and Lovers* and *The House in Clewe Street* ends with the movement of the respective heroes toward the city, which symbolizes a renewal of spirit. For Paul Morel, the movement toward the city symbolizes a rejection of the oppressive hold that his memories of his mother have upon him. This one single act foreshadows his career as an artist. For Gabriel Galloway, however, the decision to return to Dublin means that he has accepted the social and moral conventions of Castlerampart and their extreme manifestation in his Aunt Theresa. Rather than walking the razor's edge between the rigidity of his childhood and the laxity of his recent life with Sylvester, Gabriel surrenders to the narrowness and confinement of the middle-class values he will inherit along with his grandfather's property—as soon as he pays whatever penalty society insists upon for his social and moral error in running off with Onny.

Gabriel's decision reinforces the social conventions of *The House in Clewe Street*. Zack Bowen finds the novel successful exactly because it balances Gabriel's struggles and the value of the novel's "social code of behavior and social class system."[5] Unfortunately, by using the conclusion to reinforce society's demands, the novel loses much of its credibility. Rather than strengthening his character, Gabriel's acceptance of middle-class values is a surrender to all those things in the novel that have stifled independent thought and action. Unlike Paul Morel and Stephen Dedalus, both of whom make mistakes but keep their faith in their own visions, Gabriel finds his true self in the belief that true independence lies in the acceptance of an inheritance. In this respect, he is very much like Ernest Pontifex in *The Way of All Flesh*. Both characters, after failing miserably in their attempts to be independent, are rescued by inheritances. They are sympathetic heroes only because they are so badly treated as children. Much of that sympathy is lost, however, when both heroes are saved from failure by the very conventions that have made their lives so insufferable. The end result in each case is a character shaped to the purposes of the narrator. In *The Way of All Flesh*, the author's overriding demand for vengeance eventually destroys the credibility of the narrative and the novel's hero. In *The House in Clewe Street*, the same unfortunate situation occurs because the middle-class values of Castlerampart assume more importance than the genuine hopes and needs of the individual. Instead of striking a balance, *The House in Clewe Street* affirms the narrow conventions of the Irish middle class and in the bargain dooms its hero to mediocrity.

III   Mary O'Grady

If *The House in Clewe Street* is Mary Lavin's *Bildungs-Roman*, then *Mary O'Grady* is her *Mutter-Roman*. The tragedies of the O'Grady family are viewed primarily in terms of their effect upon Mary O'Grady. She is the strong maternal figure in a family which includes her husband, Tom, and five children. The chapters of the novel are named after different members of the family, but the key to the novel's structure is the way in which each event in the O'Grady history falls into place as part of the destiny of Mary O'Grady.[6] Because the third-person narrative voice in *Mary O'Grady* reflects the perspective of the central character, it is less formal and more personal than the voice in *The House in Clewe Street*. In this respect, Mary Lavin's point of view in *Mary O'Grady* is much closer to her short stories than her first novel. The end result is that *Mary O'Grady* has at least the opening advantage of a narrative that reflects the central character's thoughts and feelings.

The opening chapter in *Mary O'Grady,* significantly entitled "Mary," establishes the maternal character, country background, and early married life of Mary Lavin's heroine and namesake. Mary and Tom O'Grady live in Dublin at the turn of the century. Tom, who has the name of Mary Lavin's father, is Dublin bred, but Mary retains the simplicity and naturalness of the country life of her girlhood days. Her role as a mother figure, worshiped by her husband and children, is underlined by the way in which her years with Tom are intertwined with the birth of her children: "In the early years of their marriage their children came to Mary and Tom as seasonally as the flowers came up in their fields, or as the stock in the pasture at home had their young to run at foot with them."[7] Her function as a life-sustaining force is also established early through Tom's pride in the good health that characterizes Mary's pregnancies and confinements, and in "the fact that, unlike the pale, papery wives of other men, out of the fullness and plentitude of her body she had nourished her children" (p. 18).

The atmosphere of the opening chapter reflects the joy Mary

shares with Tom during the years of the births of their children. The
one single event that symbolizes Mary's happiness is her daily visit
to a vacant lot near the bank of the Grand Canal. Usually accom-
panied by one child in hand and another in a perambulator, the
children's identities changing with the passing years, Mary enjoys
the pleasure of a meadow in the middle of the city that reminds her
of her childhood in Tullamore. These moments, because they fuse
the deep emotional satisfaction she feels as a mother and the fond
memories she has of a golden, innocent past, are as perfect as any
she experiences in the novel. They represent a state of bliss that will
soon be shattered by tragedy.

Even though the opening scenes in "Mary" are happy ones for
the novel's heroine, they also foreshadow future tragedies. Mary's
concern for the safety of her children is particularly revealing. She
has a great fear during her childbearing years that some physical
harm will come to her children once they are out of her grasp.
When Patrick, her first child, is born, Mary is afraid to let one of her
neighbors hold him: "More than anything in the world, even when
she held him tightly in her own arms, she was afraid of his falling.
She heard stories—Oh! She couldn't bear to think of them now that
she had a baby of her own soft and pulsing in her arms" (p. 6).
Later, when her children are older and able to walk, her fear shifts
from the carelessness of a neighbor to the great danger lurking in
railroad stations. In one episode, which echoes Mary Lavin's
favorite scene from Tolstoy's *Anna Karenina,* while the family waits
for an excursion train to Bray, a gust of wind blows Angie's hat onto
the rails in front of an onrushing engine. Mary's dread that her
daughter will break away from her is so great that she screams in
terror, even though nothing has happened to the child: "Oh, the
terror she felt that day, and the terrible feeling that came over her
as she saw the familiar little straw hat lying on the line in front of
that engine that was advancing so relentlessly upon it. It would
have been just the same if it had been the child herself that lay
upon the line in front of it" (p. 21).

Mary O'Grady also fears that some day she will lose her children
because of their natural curiosity about the outside world. Though
not as intense as her terror of physical harm, her concern with their
growing fascination with the world beyond the protective family
circle is closely related to her earlier fear. She realizes that any decision taking a son or daughter beyond her immediate care deprives
her of the chance to protect the child from harm. Worrying more

about her sons than her daughters, who will have husbands to care for them, Mary is particularly sensitive to Patrick's early interest in trains and his fascination with the distant mountains. Though Patrick, after a holiday with his father, tells her that the mountains, viewed up close, are nothing more than ordinary fields, it is only a matter of time, however, until Patrick grows old enough to seek other mountains, and Ellie and Angie, the oldest girls, mature enough to dream of a home and children of their own. During a moment so filled with tender joy that she sheds tears of happiness, Mary tells Tom that " 'I'd better save my tears. . . . A day may come when I'll need them worse than today' " (p. 25).

In "Tom," the second chapter of *Mary O'Grady*, events suddenly shift from the blissful to the tragic. There is a happy atmosphere in much of the chapter because of the introduction of the young suitors, Bart and Willie; but Patrick's decision to seek his fortune in America and Tom's sudden death dramatically alter the emotional life of the O'Grady family. At first, the chapter seems curiously misnamed because of Tom's relatively insignificant role in his daughters' courtships. His death, however, causes the first real crisis in the O'Grady family: "They were a set of individuals, she thought with panic, herself included. The thread that had bound them into a family was broken" (p. 85). Within this tragic and uncertain atmosphere, Mary makes other discoveries and decisions that, unknown to her, prepare the way for future tragedies. At first, her discoveries, rather than tragic, seem to offer some compensation for the loss of Tom. She learns that Ellie, her oldest daughter, has accepted a ring from Bart and that Ellie's nature is entirely different from her own. What she realizes about Ellie is that she will always retain a "core of enmity in her heart against all men" (p. 91). Whereas Mary knows that she stopped being a woman first when she became a mother, she believes that Ellie "will always be a woman first, and a wife and a mother afterwards" (p. 91).

Mary's knowledge of Ellie's engagement restores her faith in the continuity of the family. When she finds out about Patrick's desire to emigrate to America, however, Mary senses a new threat to the emotional stability of the family. Even though Patrick insists that he has changed his mind because of his father's death, his decision lacks any real conviction. Once again, Patrick's restlessness, his spirit of adventure, casts a shadow upon Mary's heart. She recognizes, however, that her old fears cast an even greater shadow upon Patrick's life. If Patrick takes on his father's responsibilities instead of seeking his fortune in America, he will never escape the feeling of being a prisoner in his own home. Mary resolves the conflict in her own heart by encouraging Patrick to follow his plan, while asking for only one concession from her oldest son. Because of her great pride in her family, she insists that Patrick not work his way across, that he accept her offer of money for a proper passage. This way no taint of poverty will bring bad luck to the beginning of his journey, and hinder his search for happiness in America.

In "Patrick," the key event is the departure of Patrick, the eventuality that Mary, before the unexpected death of Tom, believed would be the first great sorrow of her life. As in the previous chapter, a new narrative thread also appears seemingly to belie the title of the novel's third chapter. The courtship of Ellie and Bart actually assumes more narrative importance than Patrick's impending journey. For the first time in the novel, the third-person point of view shifts from Mary's thoughts and feelings to those of her oldest daughter. The emotional differences Mary discovered between herself and Ellie now become a part of the narrative strategy of the novel. This shift from a maternal to a more womanly (no Shavian pun intended) perspective gives Mary Lavin the opportunity to explore Ellie's emotional experience as she becomes more and more committed to a life with Bart. Ostensibly, until the excitement of Patrick's departure, the main narrative interest is the young couple's search for a house. Out of their search, however, Ellie learns a great deal about the hidden passions that attract and divide the sexes: "How strange it all was: how little part one seemed after all to take in determining the course of one's own life. What a matter of hazard and chance it was. And how different, in so many hundreds and thousands of ways, was a man from a woman" (pp. 111 - 12).

After the narrative diversion into Ellie's emotional adventures and discoveries, the perspective returns to Mary O'Grady and her great sorrow. Ironically, other than Patrick's brief moment of secret agony when he realizes how dear his mother is to him, there is no heartrending scene at the moment of parting. Everything happens so quickly that Mary never has the opportunity for one last expression or gesture of maternal love and wisdom:

And out of all the incidents that led up to that moment, and which she had borne with such calmness and fortitude, this one, single incident alone seemed incomprehensible: that the train had begun to move. He was gone, and she had said nothing to him. All the fears that had filled her heart in the past two weeks, all the anxieties that kept her tossing wakeful in her bed at night, returned now, and threw her into a panic. The dangers against which he should have been warned, the exhortations and admonitions that should have been contained in her last parental words with him! Why had she said none of them? (p. 128)

The opening scene of the next chapter and its title, "Bart and Ellie," strongly suggest that some compensation exists to ease the sorrow of Patrick's absence. The festive atmosphere and Bart's talent for drawing Mary's attention away from her recent loss to the approaching marriage quickly establish a pattern of hope and promise. The only discordant note during the family's happy gathering is sounded in a conversation about traveling between Mary and her daughters' suitors. The intent of their remarks is to assure Mary that the dangers of icebergs and storms are a thing of the past. Knowing that Bart and Willie are engineering students, she respectfully accepts their view. Unfortunately, her old fears are revived when Bart casually mentions the possibility that people may soon be crossing the ocean "by aeroplane," and that someday she may receive a letter from Patrick telling her of his coming home by air. As for the narrative, Bart's enthusiasm not only serves as a reminder of Mary's early dread of her children suffering some terrible fall, it also foreshadows the next tragedy in the O'Grady family. No subtle narrative link between the fears of the past and the horrors to come, however, is sufficient in itself to prepare for the excessiveness of the next catastrophe.

The terrible fate of the two young couples, while imposing a tremendous burden on Mary O'Grady, who has already suffered the sudden death of her husband and the emigration of her oldest son to America, seriously strains the credibility of the novel. The foreshadowing of the tragedy and the wholesale nature of the event itself introduces an intrusive sense of narrative manipulation into the novel. The relationship between narrator and central character becomes more biblical than aesthetic as Mary Lavin now plays God to Mary O'Grady's Job.

Exactly three weeks and a day after Patrick leaves for America, Bart arrives at the O'Grady house with the "good news" that an English company has brought a few planes to Dublin and is offering pleasure rides as a way of advertising air travel. Overcoming her initial horror because of the excitement of the young people, Mary

makes "the suggestion that altered everything" (p. 150). By encouraging them to go to Phoenix Park, she sets in motion the fateful
events that cause the deaths of Bart, Willie, Ellie, and Angie. Out of
the happy company that leaves for Phoenix Park, only Larry, the
youngest son, is spared, presumably so that he may bring the tragic
news of the fatal crash to his mother. Ironically, just before hearing
about the horrible accident, Mary takes an emotional inventory of
her present situation. Because she feels twice blessed by the approaching addition of Bart and Willie to her family, she decides that
her life on balance is rather fortunate. She even accepts Patrick's
absence as a new source of joy, for no longer does she have to
burden herself with the "small groundless fears" that had troubled
her since his birth. Her thoughts become so serene that she returns
in memory to the blissful end of the day at Tullamore, which she
transforms into a celebration of the universal joy of motherhood: "It
was the hour of all the day most peaceful and blessed, when all, all,
was laid to rest, and her mother lay down on her own bed secure in
the knowledge that all things in her care were safe for that night at
least" (p. 154).

At the very moment of her happiness, Mary receives one last
blessing, her first letter from Patrick. The good news in the letter
reinforces her sense of security and well-being; but almost as soon
as she finishes the letter, her state of bliss is shattered by Larry's
news of the accident. At first she does not quite grasp what Larry is
trying to tell her. When she finally understands the full truth, that
all four are dead, Mary feels the enormity of her loss in terms of the
vast "teeming city that seemed to roar around her ears all at once
with the deafening roar of water" (p. 155). This feeling of being
engulfed by the terrible, indifferent waters of life, leaves her de-
vastated. Unable to respond to this bitter stroke of fate that comes
at the very moment she was counting her blessings, she falls from
the peaceful memories of Tullamore into unconsciousness.

The next two chapters, "Larry" and "Rosie," take their titles
from the names of the O'Grady children still remaining at home.
There is little doubt of Larry's significance in the first chapter. As it
is his voice that brought the tragic news to his mother, so it is also
his words that revive her. Unconscious for three days—the biblical
parallel is obvious—Mary is summoned back to life by Larry's
spoken fear that he is to blame for all that has happened. Drawn
back to life by the realization of the emotional needs of her
youngest son, she repeats the same words, "My son," that she cried
out to Patrick as his train pulled out of the station. The words, also

spoken by David at the sight of his dead son, Absalom, end another tragic cycle in the O'Grady family. The moment itself revives the maternal strength of Mary O'Grady so that she may endure her suffering and still sustain the rapidly dwindling ranks of her family. As she tells Larry, " 'He needs me more than any of them, I thought, and after that I called your name. And now, son, let us not talk about what's past but think about what is to come' " (p. 184).

What comes is anticipated in a surprising comment Mary makes while talking about the death of her children. Up to this point in the novel, religion has played no role in the history of the O'Grady family. Suddenly, however, Mary discovers a way of accepting her great loss:

Aren't we taught to believe that we must all sooner or later be separated for a while, but that in a little while more we will be united again? Think of it Larry. Think of it: one day we will all be united again, your father and I, and Ellie and Angie. Those meetings will come first of course, but after another little while the rest of you will join us and we will all be together once more, and never, never be separated again! (p. 182)

Once religion is interjected into the plot of *Mary O'Grady*, it becomes a major factor in the lives of the O'Grady family. Its sudden importance, however, places a further strain on the credibility of the novel. In the next episode, Father Dowling, described as Larry's old friend, tells his protégé that God has selected him for the religious life. Larry suddenly sees his soul unfolding to its purpose, and Mary, when informed of Father Dowling's conversation with her son, proclaims the glorious goodness of God's ways. The narrative, already struggling under the load of a rapidly mounting number of family tragedies, now interjects, with a complete absence of irony, the strong religious faith of the central character, even though this faith has not even been hinted at in the first half of the novel. An ironic viewpoint, such as the one in *A Portrait of the Artist as a Young Man*, would have established a proper distance between religion and the fate of the central character. In this way, the strong appearance of the Church at this point in the novel would be another external force acting upon Mary's life, and a new potential threat to her natural maternal instincts. Rather, because of Mary's suddenly strong religious sentiment and the novel's great dependence upon the central character for its narrative perspective, the problem of sentimentality increases as the reader enters the second half of the novel.

All is not glory and salvation for Mary O'Grady as she readies her son for the seminary. Her latest problem, however, has nothing to do with the new role that the Church plays in her life. Her letters from Patrick, which she sees as proof of his well-being, have been arriving less frequently. This warning sign, while foreshadowing the fact that neither God nor the narrator is done with Mary O'Grady, also exposes the bitterness still lurking in Mary's heart in spite of her maternal strength and religious faith: "The spleen that had been rising in her for a long time and which, like the twilight of smokiness and drabness that had settled on the walls of the house, was settling in her heart. Why? She did not know. She had spared neither toil nor sweat nor sacrifice, and yet life, that had been as sweet as milk and honey, was souring, hour by hour" (p. 206).

Mary O'Grady's difficulties in the next chapter are twofold. Not only does she have new problems associated with Rosie's growing pains, she also discovers that things have been going badly for Patrick. "Rosie" picks up the narrative of *Mary O'Grady* eight years after Larry enters the seminary. The basic conflict between Rosie, now eighteen, and her mother is over the direction of Rosie's future. Rosie's desire to bring some money into the house runs at cross-purposes with Mary's ambition that her daughter enter the university. While this division between mother and daughter has the potential for developing into a major cause of grief in the O'Grady family, the most serious problem for Mary literally arrives at her door. Having received word from a relative in America that Patrick is planning to return to Ireland, Mary excitedly watches for his arrival. Her anticipation, however, is dampened by her concern that Patrick, whose letters have stopped, did not write himself to tell her the good news. When she returns from a shopping trip with Rosie and finds Patrick standing in front of her house, she learns in a matter of minutes why her oldest son stopped writing.

Mary has correctly suspected that in some way Patrick's troubles in America have something to do with the failure of the stock exchange. One of the most curious features of *Mary O'Grady* is that in the thirty-year history of the family the only two major historical events that play some role in the plot are prohibition and the stock-market crash—this in spite of the fact that the novel takes place in Dublin during the years of the infamous lockout, the Easter rising, and the Irish civil war. The devastating effect of Patrick's failure to earn great wealth in America is immediately apparent in his strange, withdrawn behavior. The narrative, by shifting from

Mary's perspective to Rosie's at the critical moment of Patrick's return, focuses on Rosie's fear and confusion. Because her brother is unresponsive and her mother's cheerful tone false, Rosie knows that something is wrong. She fails to understand the nature of Patrick's silence, however, until she suddenly discovers that he acts like a victim of some terrible ordeal. Once she realizes this, Rosie knows why her mother, in the face of the tremendous strain of the moment, is so animated by Patrick's arrival: "He was home: safe between the walls of the house where he was born, within sight, within call, within reach of her arms" (p. 238).

In "Patrick," the novel's perspective returns to Mary as the harsh realities of her son's mental illness begin to weigh heavily upon her joy at his return. At first, she experiences a wonderful interlude of bliss when Patrick seems to recover his sanity and speaks to her of his plans for their future together. Unfortunately, by the time Larry returns from the seminary, Patrick drifts back into his listless state. Larry, diagnosing his brother's condition as a severe case of melancholia, urges his mother to call the doctor, thus precipitating another tragic ordeal for her. Initially, all her maternal instincts rebel against the idea of sending her son to an institution. She defies Larry with all the natural power and authority of her role in the family: "At this moment he realized she was not a person; she was a force, against which he felt powerless to contend" (p. 274). With all the "cunning purpose of motherhood" (p. 275), she gives reason after reason for keeping Patrick at home. She cannot, however, overcome her own knowledge of the terrible influence that Patrick's condition is having on Rosie. Larry also warns her that Patrick could harm himself if not given proper care. Finally, submitting to Larry's common sense, she accepts a second and far more painful separation from the child that she loves more than all the others.

Mary O'Grady's tragic ordeals hardly end with Patrick's commitment to a mental institution. Still ahead are Rosie's unhappy marriage, Larry's dismissal from the seminary, and her own declining health. "Rosie and Frank" resumes the struggle between Mary and her daughter over Rosie's future plans. Desiring that Rosie have what she was unable to give the other children, Mary wants her daughter to enter the university. Rosie, however, persuades her mother that the money would be wasted, quickly proving her point by finding a position as an assistant in a small library. Once this is accomplished, the struggle between mother and daughter takes a new and more dangerous direction. Rosie's growing involvement with Frank Esmay causes a greater split than ever with her mother. Mary, instinctively sensing that Frank, representing a different social class and attitude, will have a disturbing influence upon Rosie's life, desperately tries to discourage her from seeing him. Fearing Tom's belief that Rosie's face would be her fortune may prove a bitter prophecy, she decides that this time she will not allow fate to deal another tragic blow to her family: "All my life, she thought, I have suffered things to happen to me without protest. This is the first time that I ever tried to take things into my own hands" (p. 322). Ironically, her decision to confront Frank with his philandering backfires. Her strategy pushes Frank into a marriage with Rosie.

In "Larry" the new crisis is Larry's return from the seminary as a spoiled priest. Very little of this chapter is told from Mary's perspective. Instead, the narrative shifts to Larry's thoughts about his dismissal and his dread of telling his mother. Thus the crisis is experienced from his point of view. One thing quickly learned is that Larry has been dismissed because of the authorities' fear that his health may not be strong enough for the rigors and pressures of the priesthood. Their decision seems to be unfairly based upon Patrick's illness rather than Larry's qualifications. Any possibility, however, of a dramatic change in attitude toward the Church on the part of Larry or his mother is quickly ended by Larry's conviction that the action is just and fair. His real concern is the terrible effect that his return will have upon his mother: "Oh poor Mother, he thought. To think that I should be the one to wound you deepest of all! I that would have done anything on earth for you; I who loved you so much more than anyone—Patrick or Ellie or Angie or Rosie" (p. 335).

Larry does find a way of sparing Mary from the ordeal of being the mother of a spoiled priest. Assisted by an inspiration from God, he decides to join the foreign missions. When he finally confronts her with the news of his dismissal, he has such a look of peace and happiness that his mother is awestricken rather than disappointed. The possibility that his ordination will happen far away where she will not be able to see it is more than compensated for by her feeling that her son has finally found his true role in life. What she sees in his heart fills her with a deep love and compassion that she has not felt since the first years of her marriage. For one of the few times in *Mary O'Grady*, its long-suffering heroine achieves a measure of bliss that helps her transcend her tragic life. Significant-

ly, it is her simple faith in God and the teachings of the Church that
inspire this moment of happiness.

There is something of a turning away from tragedy in "Rosie and
Frank" and "Larry." Once Mary accepts Patrick's institutionaliza-
tion as the best possible life for her son, she feels that each of her
remaining children has gained some protective sanctuary to shield
them from disappointment and great loneliness. In "Mary and
Rosie," however, the troubles return for Mary Lavin's long-
suffering Irish mother. The last chapter opens eight years after
Rosie's marriage. It immediately establishes her marital difficulties
as the latest and final ordeal for Mary O'Grady. Now in her fourth
decade of suffering, Mary senses that Rosie's problem has
something to do with the fact that her daughter has not had any
children. She also realizes, as a pain in her shoulder worsens, that
she will not live much longer; but because Rosie may need a refuge,
she asks God to spare her for a few more years.

How literally Mary anticipates her life after death is evident in
her worries about her burial and the reunion with her family in "the
next world." One of her great concerns is being buried in Glasnevin
rather than in Tullamore. She considers using the savings, which
have taken on so many different values and purposes during the
O'Grady history, to pay for her funeral in Tullamore. Yet she knows
that her place, even in death, is beside her husband and children:
"Where they lie, I belong, she thought. And where I belong, I shall
go. When I meet them, I want to have nothing to regret" (p. 357).
Her decision suddenly inspires a simple and troubling vision of "the
heavenly fields." Not surprisingly, the fields resemble those of her
childhood days in Tullamore. What perplexes her, however, is the
thought of literally seeing her children and her own mother. She
wants a complete paradise of body and soul, and she worries about
the physical appearance of the soul. Disturbed by the possibility
that she will see her mother as an old and ailing woman, she is even
more troubled by the prospect that her children will appear to her
as adults: "Not like that, oh God! If I am to see the children again,
let them be as they were long ago; let them be as they were when
they were small" (p. 360).

This nightmarish vision of a paradise without the simple joys of
motherhood is ended by Rosie's desperate need for her mother in
this world. Mary's long and enduring role as mother is tested one
last time by Rosie's decision to leave her husband. First, she has to
contend with Rosie's desire to blame fate for the failure of her

marriage. Challenged by her daughter's bitter complaint that the
O'Gradys are an unlucky family, Mary rejects any thoughts of
bitterness or despair by showing that she has reconciled herself to
God's will. After hearing about Frank's "Campaign" to undermine
his wife's will and Rosie's fear that she has Patrick's weakness, Mary
also dismisses the idea of some inherited physical or mental
weakness in the family. Instead she again accepts Rosie into her
bosom as nothing more complicated than a soft and vulnerable
child. Finally and incredibly, remembering how the birth of each
new child saved her from loneliness, Mary performs what amounts
to a miracle of motherly love and compassion. Pointing to Rosie's
great loneliness, she tells her daughter that it is God's way of
preparing her for a new burden: "It was just then, while they stared
at each other, that, deep in her body, Rosie felt a soft flutter like the
flutter of a young bird's wings; a feeling she had never felt before in
all her life, but which she understood as truly as the beat of her
heart: it was the first stirrings of a life imprisoned within her" (p.
384).

Mary's miraculous discovery of Rosie's pregnancy not only saves
her daughter's marriage, it assures the continuation of the O'Grady
family. The expected child also allows Mary to pass on the hopes
and burdens of motherhood to her daughter. Once this is accomplished, she turns again to her vision of the next world with a
new assurance that she will spend eternity reliving the golden days
of motherhood: " 'That's all I'd ask of God for all Eternity, just to
see you all again, and look at your faces forever and ever' " (p. 390).
And, as her vision takes on a new strength and radiance, Mary
O'Grady, like a badly sentimentalized Anna Livia Plurabelle, quietly drifts away. After all her tragic ordeals, she dies in a state of pure
grace, believing that the pregnancy of her daughter reaffirms the
maternal values that have sustained her throughout her life.

Mary's blissful death brings an end to her worldly sufferings, and
strongly suggests that she has not suffered in vain. The credibility of
Mary O'Grady, however, has been so stretched by the rapid fre-
quency of the family's tragedies that no aesthetic bliss balances the
spiritual bliss of the novel's heroine. Tom's death is acceptable as a
shocking but natural tragedy within the history of the family, but,
when Ellie, Angie, and their sweethearts, are killed in the plane
crash, the tragic events seem more manipulation than natural
history. After Tom's early death, Angie and Ellie's tragic accident,
Patrick's mental illness, Larry's failure, and Rosie's marital

problem, *Mary O'Grady* emerges as a maternal version of the story of Job. Unfortunately, it lacks the objectivity and complexity of the biblical story or the modern variations that have appeared in drama and fiction.

Mary O'Grady does develop a strong spiritual message about the enduring values of motherhood, but the strong dose of religion in the second half of the novel further damages the credibility of the novel. As Mary's religious beliefs grow in significance, the narrative voice, assuming the maternal perspective throughout most of the novel, becomes so sympathetic to her simple view of life that the point of view collapses into sentimentality. Unlike Flaubert, who maintains narrative objectivity in *Un Coeur Simple* while treating a character similar to Mary O'Grady in her simple religious values, Mary Lavin allows the narrative voice to fall into a subjective role in the novel. That flaw, along with the intrusive manipulation of the O'Grady history, spoils a novel that had the potential of expanding the successful techniques of her short stories. Mary Lavin's feeling that her two long novels should have been broken up into "the few short stories they ought to have been in the first place" is particularly relevant as a measurement of the value of *Mary O'Grady*.[8]

Her second and last novel, lacking the classical form of *The House in Clewe Street*, loses control of plot and sentiment. Yet it does have a more relaxed point of view, and its central character is far less obnoxious than the shortsighted Gabriel Galloway. Within the diverse strengths and weaknesses of the two novels are the ingredients of one very fine novel—or, as Mary Lavin has already pointed out, the materials for a few good short stories.

CHAPTER 4

The Middle Period:
The Story with a Pattern

IN the early years of her career, Mary Lavin wrote stories carefully designed to allow the reader to experience the emotional reality of her characters' lives. Her collections published in the 1950s, however, contain many stories that rely more on patterns of writing that impose the truth upon her characters and readers. "A Single Lady," "The Convert," and "A Tragedy" are successful in creating an impression of reality, but stories with surprise endings and intrusive narrators are more typical of these collections. Though well written, her patterned stories lack the fine balance of her early stories. In the 1950s, Mary Lavin also wrote a number of stories about the same character or family. Five stories from this period portray the Grimes family and collectively embody Mary Lavin's most ambitious attempt to explore the emotional reality of middle-class Irish life. The Grimes-family saga also anticipates the critical cycle of widow stories and the recurring appearance of Vera Traske, Mary Lavin's autobiographical heroine, in her later collections.

I   The Story with a Pattern

"A Story with a Pattern" is one of the few stories that makes a direct statement on the purpose of Mary Lavin's art. The story was published in 1951 but actually written in October 1939, at the very beginning of her career. "A Story with a Pattern" tells a story within a story. The narrator, a writer obviously modeled after her creator, is introduced at an afternoon party to a middle-aged man who has read some of her stories. At first he urges her to devote herself full time to a writing career. He tempers his compliment, however, with a sharp criticism of the limitations of her work. In his opinion, her stories " 'in their present form, good as they are, will never appeal to a man . . . because a man wants something with a bit of substance to it, if you know what I mean? A man wants something a bit more thick, if you understand.' "[1] More specifically, he tells her that her stories have hardly any plot and her endings are bad because nothing is ever concluded. She defends her stories by pointing out that life has little plot and tends to break off in the middle; but he argues that the reader expects the writer to offer a diversion from life's chaos by revealing some purpose to a story, some relation between cause and effect.

The issue between writer and critic now becomes the definition of truth. The writer's argument that imposing a pattern upon her story would distort the truth is countered by the critic's view that thousands of times life's incidents reveal a clear and well-marked pattern. When challenged to offer one such incident, the critic reluctantly assumes the role of storyteller. He narrates the tale of Murty Lockwood, a wealthy landowner born with clubfeet. Because of his affliction, Murty never feels accepted by the town. When he courts and wins Ursula Merrick, an intelligent woman of deep and quiet beauty, he believes, as does the town, that she marries him for his money. Ursula's love for Murty, however, is as deep and quiet as her nature. She even withholds the fact of her pregnancy from him for several months to shorten the time of his waiting. Unfortunately, Ursula's strategy backfires. Murty, seeing a sinister motive in her thoughtfulness, accuses her of carrying another man's child. His action shocks Ursula into a premature labor that leads to the death of mother and child. Murty, a man with no faith in his wife's love, is finally given undeniable proof of her faithfulness. The stillborn child has clubfeet.

The critic turned storyteller now returns to his original role. He tells the writer to publish his story with a pattern, for it is bound to make her a success. She remains adamant, however, in her faith in her own approach to writing. When asked why, she explains that she " 'won't always be able to find stories like this to tell. This was only one incident. Life in general isn't rounded off like that at the edges; out into neat shapes. Life is chaotic; its events are unrelated; its . . .' " (p. 103). The exasperated gentleman can only ask her to refrain from stating "that nonsense again" (p. 103). To prevent any further possibility, he casually walks away.

When Mary Lavin wrote "A Story with a Pattern" in 1939, she, like the writer in her story, was receiving advice, encouragement, and some criticism. Lord Dunsany, one of her earliest admirers, was also one of her early advisers. Though he wrote in his preface to *Tales from Bective Bridge* that he had very little advice to give her because of her great skill, he suggested, in their private letters, that she needed a little more story in her writing and even recommended O. Henry as a guide. Robert W. Caswell believes that "A Story with a Pattern" was not meant to be Mary Lavin's "direct answer to Dunsany's mild concern for the tenuous narrative movement in some of her work," but "it does reveal that Miss Lavin was fully aware of the objections to one kind of story that she was writing."[2] Her early collections show that she rejected Dunsany's advice to include a little more story to get a better "grip upon the reader." A typical story in *Tales from Bective Bridge, The Long Ago,* and *The Becker Wives* has an intrinsic design formed out of the emotional truth of its central character. The appearance of "A Story with a Pattern" in *A Single Lady,* however, clearly demonstrates "how capable she was of writing a story with a very strong and clearly demarcated plot line."[3]

II   A Single Lady and Other Stories

The majority of stories in *A Single Lady* strongly suggest a change of direction in Mary Lavin's writing. "A Single Lady" and "The Convert" continue the trend of her early work, but several others are clearly stories with a pattern. "A Single Lady" skillfully weaves the emotional drama of an aging spinster who struggles against the intimate alliance between her elderly father and their coarse household drudge. With mocking echoes of Cinderella, the story exposes the inadequacy of the daughter's delicate sensibilities against the gross sensuality of the servant in her battle to win back her father's affection. "The Convert," the first of the Naida Paston stories, observes the bitter fate of a young man who goes against his own nature by rejecting the gentle and reserved Naida and marrying the sensual Mamie. The emotional conflict, heightened by religious differences, reaches a climactic pitch when Naida dies; but no tragedy of nature frees Elgar from the grim reality of his marriage to Mamie. Both stories develop the tragic theme of opposed natures within a carefully controlled point of view that reflects the temperament of the central character. Unfortunately, "A Single Lady" and "The Convert," the most satisfying stories in the collection, are exceptions to the story telling pattern in *A Single Lady.*

"Posy" is a strong example of the type of story that dominates *A Single Lady*. The fictional critic of "A Story with a Pattern" would have little trouble appreciating this story within a story of a refined and sensible young man who returns to the village where his mother was born to discover some part of the truth about her humble background. What he encounters is the memory of a timid and dried-up shopkeeper. Never knowing the identity of the young man, the shopkeeper tells him of his near involvement with a young servant girl he playfully called Posy, and how he narrowly escaped marriage with a girl from an inferior social class. The difference in natures between the timid shopkeeper and the vital Posy resembles the pattern of Mary Lavin's earlier stories, but there is a truth imposed on "Posy" that makes it more like "A Story with a Pattern."

As Daniel, the old shopkeeper, tells his story, it becomes more and more apparent from the young man's comments that he is Posy's son. Because he never realizes this truth himself, Daniel unwittingly reveals the mistreatment Posy suffered from his family because he liked her, and how they practically forced her to leave the village to protect Daniel from his own foolishness. His curiosity about Posy's fate is never satisfied by the mysterious young man, but satisfying the desire for a good story is clearly a factor as "Posy" winds to its conclusion. The impressive bearing of the young man that Daniel assumes to be a Dublin solicitor clearly suggests that Posy found happiness and prosperity after leaving the town's narrow world. Because the careful reader is rewarded with this insight, his enjoyment of the story goes beyond experiencing the mean and narrow existence of a man who missed his one chance for love. Knowing that Posy did well for herself, that she triumphed over Daniel and his family, makes it easy for the reader to condemn Daniel and appreciate this satisfying situation. Unfortunately, because Mary Lavin imposes a clever ending upon the story, the higher satisfaction of sharing the emotional drama of her characters is greatly diminished. In stories like "A Cup of Tea" and "A Happy Death," her readers have the opportunity to experience the truth. In "Posy" they are told the truth.

Several other stories in *A Single Lady* create the same effect as "Posy." In each case, the cleverness of the writer in arranging the plot and creating a surprise ending diverts the reader's attention away from whatever experience the story offers into the simple and often painful truths of the human heart. "The Small Bequest" and "The Pastor of Six Mile Bush" are particularly dependent upon a surprise ending for their success. In "The Small Bequest" there is a curious strain in the otherwise perfect relationship between Adeline Tate, a member of a wealthy and distinguished family, and Emma Blodgett, her female companion for twenty-seven years. After carefully observing the elderly pair, the first-person narrator concludes that Miss Tate secretly resents being called Aunt Adeline by Miss Blodgett, even though the name is freely used by all the members of the Tate family. Miss Tate, who never corrects the indiscretion, believes that Miss Blodgett's familiarity is a gross intrusion upon her family's dignity and an outrageous effort by a common person to claim membership. There are some ironic echoes of the biblical story of Eden in "The Small Bequest." The elderly ladies spend their days in Miss Tate's perfect garden designed for "the different needs of bird and beast and butterfly" (p. 112). The chief interest of the narrator, however, is in identifying the lurking serpent that destroys their blissful relationship.

After discovering the source of "Aunt Adeline's" bitterness, the narrator's final task is relating the nature of Miss Tate's revenge on her too faithful companion. The narrator's fear that Miss Tate will withdraw her small bequest for Emma Blodgett is well-founded, but her discovery of the manner in which the bequest is denied creates the story's surprise ending. When the narrator returns from her travels, she finds Miss Tate dead, and poor Miss Blodgett living in near poverty. First believing that Miss Tate removed the small bequest from her will, she quickly learns that Miss Blodgett lost her legacy, which was very generous, because Miss Tate identified her only as her "fond niece Emma" (p. 136) in the will. Miss Tate's revenge is complete because Miss Blodgett never realizes that she is a victim of revenge. She believes that "Aunt Adeline" made an error out of an excess of love. Only the narrator is aware of the irony of the words: " 'Poor Aunt Adeline! Poor Aunt Adeline' " (p. 138).

Though the subject matter and final outcome of "The Pastor of Six Mile Bush" are different, the story follows the same basic pattern of "The Small Bequest." Three young men, two university students and one seminarian, set out on a journey to the small, dismal parish of Six Mile Bush to find out if the story about its pastor's gluttony is true. Told from the sympathetic perspective of Alexis, the seminary student, the story reaches its climax when the students arrive after twilight at the pastor's house. They witness what they believe is the undeniable proof of the pastor's pleasureless sin. Hidden by darkness, they gaze through a window and watch with disgust as he approaches a large joint of mutton with his long and

worn carving knife: "Then down into the bleeding centre of the
meat he drove the knife, and when he pulled it up again it was only
to hack into it in another place, until in a matter of minutes the
joint was reduced to a heap of rough hunks of meat, and except for
some scraps of grizzle and fat, nothing remained of the great
haunch but the bare bone" (p. 217).

The surprising twist to the climax of "The Pastor of Six Mile
Bush" comes when one of the students inadvertently hits the window with his fist. To their astonishment the pastor opens the window, and hands the platter of meat to his "friends," telling them
that they know what to do with it. Their confusion is quickly ended,
however, when they discover that they are surrounded by the poor
and hungry children of the parish. Once the students recognize the
pastor's error, they understand the truth about his secret gluttony.
For Alexis, whose commitment to the priesthood is at stake, the
dread expectancy of seeing the inhuman pastor of Six Mile Bush is
supplanted by his vision of a religious man who possesses "the
strange inhuman quality of those who are not only extremely old,
but who are already withdrawn in spirit and desire from normal
dealings with their human kind" (p. 221). For the reader, the
climactic meeting is both surprising and satisfying. Unfortunately,
the sudden turnabout, once again, imposes a truth upon the reader.
The discovery of the pastor's true nature gives a definite purpose to
"The Pastor of Six Mile Bush," but it also implies that the purpose
of fiction is to offer a statement about life rather than the experience of living.

"A Woman Friend" and "A Gentle Soul" are not dependent
upon surprise endings for their success, but they qualify in a
different way as stories with a pattern. Each story "adds a bit of
substance" to its plot by relying upon an unexpected physical event
to create an emotional crisis. In "A Woman Friend" a doctor's hard-
earned reputation is threatened by one critical error. Even though
he saves himself from public disgrace with a lie, his comfortable
relationship with Bina, his "woman friend," is dramatically altered.
One of the ironies of "A Woman Friend" is that its crisis develops
out of the very circumstances that have secured the doctor his
public recognition. His success is based on a reputation for hard
work and incredibly long hours of duty. His only diversion is the
time spent in Bina's secure company. After his usual late-evening
visit, he manages to drive safely to his lodgings, but falls asleep at
the wheel of his car once he parks it in front of his house. In his ex-

hausted state, he sleeps until the morning. Unfortunately, the hospital has been desperately trying to call him all night for his assistance in treating a young boy who has become seriously ill. By the time he answers the call, the patient is near death and dies shortly thereafter.

Once the doctor has a chance to talk to Bina, he gains control of himself. By blaming the hospital for negligence because they failed to send someone to his rooms, he overcomes his professional crisis. When questioned at the inquiry by the lawyer of the dead boy's mother, he testifies that he was in his rooms when the hospital tried to reach him. The lie saves his public career, but it also marks the beginning of a dramatic change in his personal life. A doctor who takes pride in the coldness of his profession, he has no problem with his private conscience. He does, however, have a new problem in his relationship with Bina. In his one weak moment when he turned to her for support, he felt so dependent upon her belief in him that he asked her to marry him. Thus his brief professional crisis, overcome by placing his public reputation over his private integrity, leads to an irreversible change in his personal life. His new intimacy with his woman friend is contrary to his cold and aloof nature: "If he had kept his head he would have known that everything would be all right. It was a little cloud that blew up in a clear sky and after a few days it had blown over. And now everything would be the same as ever—only for Bina" (p. 178).

In "A Gentle Soul," the story within a story of the secret emotional relationship between Rose Darker, a farmer's daughter, and Jamey Morrow, the hired man, ends tragically with Jamey's accidental death. The event also forces Rose into a public lie that exposes her timid nature as it denies her love for Jamey. "A Gentle Soul" opens with Rose, the inside narrator, reflecting upon her bitterness toward her sister, Agatha, whose burial service she has just attended. The occasion of Agatha's death and burial also brings into sharp focus Rose's painful memory of Jamey Morrow's death. Though years have passed since the tragedy, her memory is as strong as the hatred she feels for her sister. Jamey's love was not only the one joy of her life, it also symbolized the difference between Rose's nature and that of her sister and father. The reason Agatha so deeply resented Rose's secret sweetheart, other than the fact that he paid more attention to her sister, was that Jamey represented the wrong class of people. The sense of the social differences between farmer and common laborer was so strong in

Agatha and her father that Rose never openly admitted her feelings toward Jamey, accepting instead a shadowy relationship of secret exchanges and discreet glances, even after Jamey strongly hinted that they should run away together. When Jamey was killed by a mare that tossed him from a cart and trampled upon his face, Rose was left with her grief and her guilt for denying her would-be suitor. Her love, however, faced one final test, for she had to testify at the inquest. Her court statement, given after her sister and father intimated that it should reflect family and class loyalty rather than personal feelings, is not explicitly remembered, but there is no doubt she told the court about the mare's gentle nature, while never mentioning Jamey Morrow's gentleness. This final act of betrayal is what she most remembers and why she hates her sister for her conniving interference.

Both "A Woman Friend" and "A Gentle Soul" are entertaining studies of characters who deny their own natures when faced with personal crises. The act of self-betrayal, however, is caused more by an external event than by any inner conflict. In "The Widow's Son," Mary Lavin expands her concept of the story with a pattern by giving the reader the opportunity to choose between a story with an expressed truth and a story in which the truth is experienced: "This is the story of a widow's son, but it is a story that has two endings" (p. 179). The first version begins with a description of the widow's relationship with her son. For the widow, Packy is her lifeblood. She is willing to sacrifice everything for the great plans she has for him. By the time he reaches fourteen, Packy has the chance for a scholarship once he finishes his last class in school. One day in June, however, the widow's hopes and Packy's great promise come to an abrupt and tragic end. As Packy pedals his bicycle fiercely down the steep hill to his village home, he tries to avoid the squawking hens wandering about the roadway. Tragically, when one old hen, frightened by Packy's yells and the widow's flapping apron, flutters down into the middle of the road, Packy jams on his brakes and is thrown over the handlebars. At first it appears that he is not hurt seriously. By the time the widow and some of the villagers carry him into the cottage, however, they discover that he is dead.

Packy's sudden and tragic death imposes a truth upon the story about the precarious nature of the best-laid plans of mice and men, but the narrator offers her reader an alternative truth through the device of a second ending. She justifies her action by identifying

with the widow's neighbors, who wonder from time to time what
would have happened had Packy not yielded to his impulse to jam
down the brakes and had ridden boldly over the hen:

For these people knew the widow and they knew Packy, and when you
know people well it is as easy to guess what they would say and do in certain circumstances as it is to remember what they actually did say and do in
other circumstances. In fact, it is sometimes easier to invent than to
remember accurately, and were this not so two great branches of creative
art would wither in an hour: the art of the story-teller, and the art of gossip.
So, perhaps, if I try to tell you what I myself think might have happened
had Packy killed that cackling old hen, you will not accuse me of abusing
my privileges as a writer. (p. 185)

After this bit of insight into the art of storytelling, the narrator
begins the second story of the widow and her son, which in many
respects "is the same as the old" (p. 185). The basic difference
between the stories is that this time Packy does not die tragically,
but instead rides over the hen and comes to a safe stop. What
follows, however, is not the expected happy ending. The widow,
once the immediate danger to Packy has passed, reacts violently to
the loss of the hen. In front of the neighbors, attracted by the com-
motion, she lashes her son with the torn and bloody carcass, ac-
cusing him of killing the hen deliberately to avoid going to school.
When she discovers that Packy rode so furiously to tell her the
wonderful news of his scholarship, the widow struggles between her
impulse to embrace her son and her desire not to appear wrong in
her neighbors' eyes. Torn by love and pride, grief and shame, she
chooses to humiliate Packy in public. Her attitude softens once they
are alone together, but her awkward attempts to comfort him are
not enough to overcome the effect of her abusive treatment.
Because she has sacrificed so much for his education, her manners
are "as twisted and as hard as the branches of the trees" (p. 192).
Even her gestures of kindness appear harsh and cruel. When she
awakens in the morning, the widow discovers that her son is gone.
In the next few weeks, she receives letters from him in which he
says that he is not coming back to the village, but that he will pay
her back for all her troubles. In the next few years, he sends her the
money, but never a return address.

   In the last paragraph of "The Widow's Son," the narrator offers
her own judgment of the value of each ending. She has already
stated her bias for the second ending in her comment on the art of

storytelling, but she feels that the first ending also "has a certain element of truth about it" (p. 194). She suggests that all actions have a double quality, that if her readers are sincere and observant, they will follow their destined path, which, no matter how tragic, "is better than the tragedy we bring upon ourselves" (p. 194). The narrator's argument for accepting one's fate instead of inviting tragedy, while having a certain moral and spiritual appeal, is also an implied approval of the story with a pattern, which dominates *A Single Lady*.

In some unpublished statements that she made about Katherine Mansfield's fiction, Mary Lavin points out the problem that develops when a writer imposes a moral or emotional truth upon her story.[4] Katherine Mansfield, more than anything else, desired to reveal the truth about her characters. Mary Lavin feels, however, that in "Bliss" and "Miss Brill" Katherine Mansfield fell far short of her goal. The central character in "Miss Brill" is an elderly lady, similar to Mary Lavin's Miss Holland, who creates an atmosphere of excitement and fascination for herself by imagining that she plays a key role in a secret emotional drama with strangers in the park. When a young couple sits down near her, Miss Brill sees them as the hero and heroine of her imaginary play; but when she overhears the boy describe her to his girl friend as "that stupid old thing," her fragile, make-believe world is shattered.[5]

In "Bliss," a younger woman, Bertha Young, experiences a state of emotional happiness similar to Miss Brill's. Her bliss is created out of the stability of her marriage and home and her "blissful treasure" of small but tender moments which she believes are the very essence of life. Her happiness is intensified at an evening party when she stands side by side with Pearl Fulton, one of her social "finds," and shares with Pearl the exquisite, almost unearthly experience of looking upon a slender, flowering pear tree caught in a circle of moonlight. Her joy, however, is shattered when she accidentally observes her husband whispering lovingly to Pearl. Her discovery of Pearl's source of happiness destroys Bertha's delicate fabric of bliss, even though the pear tree remains "as lovely as ever and as full of flower and as still."[6]

The surprise endings of "Miss Brill" and "Bliss" have the same effect as the endings in Mary Lavin's stories with a pattern. The painful truths suddenly revealed in both stories are imposed upon the central characters by chance discoveries: a cruel statement overheard in a park, an indiscreet vow of love made in a drawing room. Mary Lavin's complaint is that this type of story, though often entertaining and well-written, denies the reader the satisfaction of experiencing the truth. The final effect in "Miss Brill" and "Bliss" is that of telling the truth to the reader.

This difference between experiencing fiction and simply being entertained and manipulated by it is, for Mary Lavin, the one way of distinguishing between the success and failure of the writer who hopes to create an impression of reality in her stories. Accordingly, she sees two other Mansfield stories, "Prelude" and "At the Bay," as more successful than "Miss Brill" and "Bliss" because they create an atmosphere of reality out of the simple experiences of the Burnell family. Rather than allowing one event to dominate the stories and become the instrument of truth, Katherine Mansfield successfully weaves a fabric of truth out of the brief moments of her characters' lives. Looking back upon her own stories after judging the value of Katherine Mansfield's fiction, Mary Lavin believes that stories like "A Cup of Tea" and "The Convert" create the same effect as "Prelude" and "At the Bay," but admits that "Posy" and "The Small Bequest," stories she came to reject, are closer in conception to "Miss Brill" and "Bliss."

III   The Patriot Son and Other Stories

The stories collected in *The Patriot Son* represent one of the oddest mixtures in the Lavin canon, though most are closer to her stories with a pattern than to her earlier fiction. "An Old Boot," "Frail Vessel," and "The Little Prince" form a trilogy of stories dealing with the Grimes family, and continue the history which begins in "A Visit to the Cemetery," a Grimes story in *A Single Lady*. "Limbo," the second Naida Paston story, suggests another link between *The Patriot Son* and *A Single Lady*. The story narrates the problems Naida, whose death is the focal point of the emotional conflict in "The Convert," encounters when she becomes the new Protestant student in a Catholic school. "The Patriot Son," the title story of the collection, is the most unusual story in the collection. It is the only Lavin story that uses the political troubles of Ireland for dramatic background. The personal difficulties of a shopkeeper in overcoming his oppressive relationship with his mother are played out upon the rebellious atmosphere of Ireland in the years leading up to the Easter rising. There is even one story, "An Akoulina of the Irish Midlands," that attempts to imitate the bitter realism of Turgenev's "The Tryst."

Point of view, a key factor in the success of Mary Lavin's earlier stories, is the cause of the most serious problems in *The Patriot Son*. In *Tales from Bective Bridge*, *The Long Ago*, and *The Becker Wives*, the narrative view, enriched from time to time by the observation of a minor character or an outside narrator, tends to reflect the perspective of the central character. In several stories in *The Patriot Son*, the narrative voice is much more involved in plot and character. At times, the narrator's familiarity with events and her willingness to judge characters and explain the story's meaning become far too intrusive. In "Scylla and Charybdis," no borrowing from Joyce's *Ulysses* intended, Pidgie, a fourteen-year-old servant girl, dreams of becoming a fine lady. She is fat and unladylike, but she has her vision. When invited to share the family's dinner, she feels that this is the beginning of her career as a fine lady; but her great expectations end abruptly when she is instructed to take her meal, Worcester dish and all, into the kitchen.

The ending of "Scylla and Charybdis," because it reflects the unreality of Pidgie's self-image and the harsh reality of social barriers, does not impose a truth upon the story. Any opportunity to conjecture upon the symbolic value of the title, however, is quickly denied by the narrative voice. Intrusively, the narrator gives an exact meaning to Pidgie's Scylla and Charybdis, thereby marring an otherwise satisfactory ending. By doing the reader's work, the concluding remarks ignore the possible relationship of Pidgie's journey between dream and reality to the title of the story. What remains is a reflection of the narrator's own cleverness. The final effect destroys the fabric of reality in "Scylla and Charybdis" in much the same manner as the narrator's comments on the two endings of "The Widow's Son" inadvertently expose the weakness of the story. *Ulysses* would be much easier to read if a specific meaning were given to the reader at the end of each episode; but the reader would have lost much of the delight of self-discovery, and the novel much of its realism, if the intricate parallels had been simplified and explained. There are disadvantages in being a Stuart Gilbert, a Frank Budgen, or the reader of a story that explains itself.

One of the reasons for the narrator's intrusive familiarity in "Chamois Gloves" is the almost fablelike atmosphere of the story. In narrative strategy "Chamois Gloves" resembles "Brother Boniface" and "A Fable," particularly in its simplistic approach to characterization. As a study of the religious mind, it offers a fabulistic counterpoint to the more realistic "The Nun's Mother." In this simple tale of the "Great Day" when five novices take their

vows for the Order, the narrator focuses on the problems of
Veronica and her guardian angel. Veronica's failure to experience
any doubts or feelings of sacrifice makes the task of her guardian
angel much too simple. The situation changes, however, when she
discovers that her sister has forgotten her chamois gloves and
decides to wash them. Suddenly her tender memories of her old life
rush back to her. As the tears stream down Veronica's face, her
guardian angel cups two tears in her hands and speeds to heaven
with the good news about Veronica's sacrifice.

Not all of the stories in *The Patriot Son* are vehicles for narrative
cleverness. "The Tragedy" is a powerful story of the emotional conflict between husband and wife created by the presence of the
wife's sister. Curiously, the plane crash, the tragedy of the title, is so
powerful in itself that it has the potential of dwarfing the personal
conflicts in the story. The crash, however, functions as a catalyst for
bringing already-existing emotional undercurrents to the surface.
"A Tragedy," told from the third-person perspective of the wife,
first develops the existing relationship between Tom and Mary (the
names suggest Mary Lavin's special interest in the story) by concen-
trating on their individual reactions to the plane crash. Tom's interest in the cause of the tragedy keeps him aloof from "base
curiosity and sensation-seeking."[7] Mary, however, while admitting
to herself that his approach is the correct one, realizes that on her
own "she would have wallowed in the gruesome details" (p. 76).
This brief revelation of the different sensibilities of Tom and Mary
occurs during the car ride to pick up her sister. Not surprisingly,
their different attitudes and emotions also manifest themselves in
their discussion of Sis. Because Tom dislikes Mary's sister, he uses
the trip to vent his resentment of her influence upon their
relationship. Emotionally torn by divided loyalties, Mary sympathizes with her older sister because of Sis's unhappy marriage and
the recent death of her husband. She knows in her heart, however,
that because of Tom she cannot play the disciple to her sister as she
did in the past: "it was not Sis who had changed, but herself, who
under Tom's influence had come to see her sister in a new light" (p.
93).

Once Tom and Mary pick up Sis, the narrative threads of "A
Tragedy" are drawn tightly together. Sis's interest in the plane
crash coincides with Mary's original inclination to wallow in the
details. Unaffected by Tom's influence over Mary, Sis keeps up a
steady chatter about the more sensational aspects of the tragedy.

Barely able to conceal his sense of outrage during the long ride home, Tom turns upon Mary when they are alone, attacking not only Sis's gross conversation but her personality in general: " 'I knew she was a fool, but I didn't realize she was such a complete one' " (p. 101). Since Tom knows that Mary still admires her sister, his comments are more of a criticism of his wife than his sister-in-law. He insists on going to bed before his wife as an emotional protest against Sis's interference in their lives. Once Mary is alone with her sister, she quickly discovers that Sis is well aware of Tom's feeling, and that she, in turn, resents Mary's loyalty to her husband: " 'Good lord, how you make me sick! You've lost every scrap of personality you ever had. You've just become a second skin for that inflated windbag' " (p. 103).

Mary's instinctive reaction is to slap Sis across the face. Her sympathies, however, are clearly with her sister because she realizes that her happy marriage gives her the emotional advantage. Mary becomes particularly upset when Sis wonders if any of the plane-crash victims made a similar mess out of their lives. While linking her personal tragedy to the larger tragedy, she also suggests that it would have been an act of mercy if she had been one of the victims. Mary is shaken by Sis's remark and the depth of her suffering: "Was it possible that Sis really envied those who had won eternal peace in that way—in that place? A deeper, and more terrible desolation took hold of her" (p. 107). When she tells Tom that Sis "wished she was dead" (p. 107), her husband, with his cold logic, restores the story's narrative distance. His sharp answer, that Sis ought to tell her woes to the dead, forces Mary to consider Sis's death wish from a larger perspective: "Not one of them—those undiscovered dead in their far-flung graves, not one of them, she knew, but would fling back, if he could, that mantle of snow and come back to it all: the misunderstandings, the worry, the tension, the cross purposes" (p. 107).

Tom's words affirm Mary's faith in her marriage, while isolating her from Sis's emotional excesses. In a larger sense, Tom's quick judgment, that life with all of its tragic consequences is preferable to death, reflects a philosophy of quiet acceptance and endurance that had a personal significance for Mary Lavin at the time "A Tragedy" was published. In her next collections, several stories focus on the emotional ordeal of widowhood, and each story explores the specific problems involved in accepting one's fate and making the first, tentative movement toward a new life. The philosophy of calm endurance in the face of great suffering not only becomes the controlling idea in these stories, it also enables Mary Lavin to maintain an objectivity in her art.

"A Tragedy" clearly illustrates the excellence Mary Lavin is capable of when she joins the craft of her earlier stories to a powerful new theme. Rather than offering the entertaining choice of two endings, "A Tragedy" skillfully reveals one sister's inability to deal with her own personal tragedy in the way she wallows in the gruesome details of the larger tragedy. The other sister, though she enjoys a happy life, shows the potential strength to endure a personal tragedy by refraining from emotional excesses. Rather than planting a fateful event into the story that forces the truth upon a character, "A Tragedy" observes and traces the emotional conflicts of its characters upon the background of a national tragedy.

None of the remaining stories in *The Patriot Son* achieves the excellence of "A Tragedy," but there are some interesting studies of human wisdom and folly relatively free from double endings, fateful accidents, guardian angels, and intrusive narrators. "The Long Holidays" and "My Vocation" are light satires of subjects Mary Lavin treated more seriously in earlier stories. In "The Long Holidays" the narrator assumes the role of a casual storyteller who occasionally comments on her tale. For the most part, however, she allows the humor to reveal itself through the outrageous fate awaiting her delicate heroine. Dolly, a comic counterpart of Miss Holland, leads a quiet and refined life until she marries the Major, a large man who plays Jeff to this female and "doll-like" Mutt. She dreams of being a generous and loving mother to Vinnie, the Major's eleven-year-old son, but she soon discovers that her vision of motherhood has not prepared her for the encounter with a real boy. To her dismay, she learns about such simple childhood realities as loud noises, smelly feet, and warts. Before she meets the Major's son, Dolly marks off the days on her calendar until he arrives for his long holidays; but after a few days of motherhood, highlighted by Vinnie's story of a school chum who removes warts by biting them off, she returns to her old task with a new sense of purpose: "Away at the bottom of the calendar, the date of Vinnie's departure was singled out as the new objective . . ." (p. 128). The cleverness of the ending, rather than disrupting the narrative, enhances the humor of the tale.

"My Vocation" is a delightfully funny story of a thirteen-year-old Dublin girl who decides to become a nun. Totally removed from the

high seriousness of "The Nun's Mother" and the fablelike simplicity of "Chamois Gloves," the story, told from the first-person point
of view, manages to poke some fun at the sisters of the Roman
Catholic Church while revealing the delightfully devilish character
of this unlikely candidate for a convent. One of Mary Lavin's most
Irish stories in dialect, character, and setting, "My Vocation" contrasts the vitality and generosity of those living in a Dublin tene-
ment with the coldness and insensitivity of the nuns representing
the Missions. Contrary, worldly, and defiant by nature, the narrator
"gets the call" when her family mocks her interest in being a nun.
When she discovers, however, that one of her future duties will be
caring for lepers, she suddenly has a moment of doubt: "And I may
as well admit straight out, that I wasn't having anything to do with
any lepers. I hadn't thought of backing out of the thing entirely at
that time, but I was backing out of it if it was to be lepers" (p. 190).

After she meets the representatives of the Missions, who seem
more interested in her personal hygiene than the health of her soul,
the narrator experiences a complete change of heart. Her diabolical
choice of a battered cab drawn by a mean-tempered horse to
transport the nuns away from the "dangers" of Dorset Street sets up
a clever and earthly fate for the nuns. When the horse bucks and
the bottom falls out of the cab, the four feet of the racing horse are
matched stride for stride by the now visible four feet of the nuns
running for dear life. The ending imposes a sweet revenge upon this
obnoxious pair of nuns, and frees the narrator for a life more in
keeping with her guile and earthliness.

As indicated in an earlier chapter, "The Patriot's Son" also uses
Irish materials for the story of Matty Conerty's brief and futile
attempt to overcome his mother's domination. Mary Lavin's main
purpose in "The Patriot Son" is to expose Matty's pathetic attempt
at heroism in the cause of the Fenians, but she also achieves a
balanced view of Ireland's political troubles. The narrative, without
making any direct statements of political loyalty, establishes a sympathetic view of the Fenian cause through the simple but effective
strategy of contrasting the shop trade of the Conertys and the
Mongons. Because of its dealings with the Royal Irish Constabulary
barracks across the road, the Conerty shop, run by Matty and his
mother, has expanded its stock. The Mongon shop, because it does
no business with the RIC, has not prospered, but it has kept the
trade and respect of the farmers from outside the town. Adding to
this contrast of the Conertys and the Mongons are the clashing per-

sonalities and political allegiances of Mrs. Conerty, who supports
the Constabulary and prevents her son from participating in the
Revival, and Sean Mongon, who becomes one of the secret leaders
of the Sinn Fein and involves Matty in a plot to burn down the
barracks. Poor Matty represents the middle ground in Irish politics.
Sean Mongon sees him as the sad symbol of oppressed Ireland:
" 'Poor Ignorant Ireland that doesn't want to be saved' " (p. 13).

Despite the early manipulation of point of view in favor of the
Sinn Fein, the objective treatment of the plan's failure and the
death of Sean Mongon achieves a balanced perspective. Mary Lavin
once mentioned that the Fenians actually burned down the
Constabulary barracks opposite the shop of her mother's people in
Athenry. By changing the outcome of the historical episode in her
story, she focuses the narrative on the human tragedy and folly involved in political and military adventures. This is accomplished
through the almost macabre twist that ends "The Patriot Son."
When Sean Mongon decides to hide behind the yard door of the
Conerty shop to escape the Constabulary, Matty puts on Sean's old
trench coat, hoping that the police will mistake him for Sean. As
they enter the hall, Matty races across the yard toward the back
shed in a feigned effort at escape. At the same moment he hears
shots being fired, he feels a sharp, ripping down the side of his bel-
ly. While falling to the ground, he experiences an "intoxication of
excitement" that seems to liberate his spirit from its narrow and suf-
focating existence. His belief that he is mortally wounded, however,
is quickly dispelled when Matty sees the Constabulary forces
gathered around Sean Mongon's crumpled body. The discovery
that his "wound" has been caused by a rusted nail that cut into him
as he was climbing the side of the shed and the shrill sound of his
mother's voice proclaiming him a witless coward who ran at the first
hint of danger restores Matty to the inescapable reality of his
pathetic life. The inescapable truth of "The Patriot Son," however,
is in its symbol of Irish history: a dead patriot betrayed by the
mother of a sincere but ineffectual citizen who represents Ireland's
one true hope. No wonder Frank O'Connor, who thinks "The
Patriot Son" suggests that the Irish Revolution was an attempt to
overthrow the Irish matriarch, wrote that Mary Lavin's one story
about Ireland's political troubles "is more than enough."[8]

There are three studies of young girls in The Patriot Son that are
not as hampered by an intrusive narrator as some of the stories in
the collection. Because "Limbo" provides some insight into the
character of Naida Paston, who also appears in "The Convert," it

has a twofold function in the Lavin canon. The story covers the period of the Paston family's arrival in Castlerampart after their long stay in Africa as lay missionaries.[9] Naida's desire for a close friend after her lonely years in Africa is complicated by the fact that she is the only Protestant student at the local school. Because she is forced to wait in a cloakroom during prayers, Naida experiences a deeper loneliness than she has ever felt before. Even an acquaintance with the bold and coarse Mamie Sully, whose role in "The Convert" is of greater significance, does little to minimize her sense of isolation. Though Naida's sensitivity, her religious background, and her early "friendship" with Mamie invite comparisons of "Limbo" with "The Convert," her childhood dilemma has an intrinsic interest in itself. Her emotional limbo touches her classmates as well as herself. Because Naida does not embrace the "one, true religion," the Catholic children "know" that she cannot go to heaven; but because they instinctively sense her gentleness, they find it difficult to imagine her going to hell. Their solution, which avoids any contradiction of their faith, and acknowledges Naida's goodness, is to consign her to Limbo. Though offering no strong condemnation of the stifling effects of Catholic dogma or suggesting no sympathetic attitude toward non-sectarianism, the story of Naida and her classmates does reveal the way in which the simple mind of the child is far more capable of flexibility and understanding than the adult mind rigidly committed to a set of ideas or rules.

"A Glimpse of Katey" does not have the broad theme of "Limbo." It observes a brief, foolish moment in the life of a young girl. Her folly is in going to bed without eating, and her fear of darkness complicates her predicament. When she tries to join her family downstairs, she runs into her angry father, who wants everyone in bed. She saves herself from a scolding by telling her father that she, too, was awakened by the noise downstairs. Her lie saves her from momentary danger, but Katey, in her fear of facing her family in the morning, senses that some elusive but important moment in her life has taken place. Told by a narrator who comments at times on the difficult relationship between the child and the adult, "A Glimpse of Katey" develops into a study of Katey's passage from her childhood fears to the real dangers of the adult world: "Around the room the shadows had grown to greater bulk than before, they lurked in every corner, but Katey was not afraid of them anymore. Now she was afraid of the morning" (p. 117).

In "An Akoulina of the Irish Midlands," the narrative voice

epitomizes the intrusive familiarity that hampers the point of view in most of the stories in *The Patriot Son*. The narrator, an artist by profession, introduces herself to the reader, and discusses the purpose of her tale. Though she admits that her Akoulina, named Lena in the story, does not resemble the beautiful peasant girl in Turgenev's "The Tryst," she implies the reason for drawing the reader's attention to Turgenev's heroine by mentioning Akoulina's rejection by Victor Alexandritch. What follows is a story, with the narrator participating as observer and minor character, of a plain but animated young woman who works as a servant at a small country hotel. She is wooed and betrayed by Andy Hackett, the local version of Turgenev's Alexandritch. The difference in religion between Protestant Lena and her Catholic lover gives Andy a way of avoiding any open commitment to her. The narrator, who accidentally discovers the trysting place of the young lovers, overhears Andy's calculating strategy of discouraging Lena from converting to his faith, ostensibly because it would offend her family, while promising her some ominously vague solution to their problem in the near future.

"An Akoulina of the Irish Midlands," in itself, is an interesting study of the seduction and betrayal of a gullible young girl by her cunning lover. The telling of the story, however, is hampered by the intrusiveness of the narrator. This problem is most evident in the narrator's awkward explanation of how she happened to stumble upon the exact place used by Lena and Andy for their tryst, and her summary of the fate of her subject: "And I did not see Lena again. I left the hotel the next morning before the maids were stirring. But I often thought of her, and of the flame that burned all day long in her heart. I wonder, but now will never know, how long before it was quenched" (p. 148). Her last comments are as artificial and confining as her opening revelation that her heroine will suffer the same fate as Turgenev's beautiful peasant girl.[10] The artificiality imposed upon "An Akoulina of the Irish Midlands" is typical of the stories with a pattern in *A Single Lady* and *The Patriot Son*. These stories are entertaining and cleverly written, but they lack the quality of most of Mary Lavin's earlier fiction, and fall short of her goal of capturing the emotional experience. Though clever enough to be popular, her middle stories, with their intrusive narrators and surprise endings, are not representative of her best fiction. In her future collections, her stories return to the form of her earlier fiction, and assume an even greater power and authority because of their mature theme.

IV *The Grimes Stories*

"A Visit to the Cemetery," the last story in *A Single Lady*, introduces the Grimes family, a group of characters representing Mary Lavin's most sustained effort to capture the atmosphere of the Irish middle class. It is the first of five Grimes-family stories, written over a period covering three collections of short stories and more than a decade of Mary Lavin's career. Augustine Martin, the first critic to identify the Grimes saga, regards "A Visit to the Cemetery" as a small masterpiece in its suggestiveness, insights, and ability "to capture the essential and characteristic rhythm of [Miss Lavin's] chosen situation."[11] The first Grimes story focuses on two sisters, Alice and Liddy, and their emotional experience while visiting their mother's grave four months after her death. The sisters' mood is influenced by the dismal condition of the old cemetery. The older and more practical Alice remembers her humiliation at the funeral because of the unkept condition of the cemetery. The younger and more sensitive Liddy is bothered by the cemetery's isolated location. When Alice reminds her that they will not be buried in the family plot if they marry, Liddy's dark mood is dispelled by her excitement and anticipation. The emotional appeal of their future marriages creates a common bond between Alice and Liddy. Their decision to visit the new cemetery reflects the brief, intense triumph of hopeful anticipation over the more melancholy emotions associated with death and isolation. The shadow of the past, represented by their mother's grave, is, for the moment, cast out by the happy vision of love and marriage. Unlike their mother's grave in the old cemetery, their imagined graves in the new cemetery symbolize the promise of lives as yet unlived and the triumph of the intuitive imagination over the restrictions of memory and fate.

The excellence of "A Visit to the Cemetery" is not achieved again in the Grimes stories, but Mary Lavin's interest in the family becomes clearer in the three Grimes stories in *The Patriot Son*. "An Old Boot" introduces Bedelia, the most dominating character in the Grimes saga. Ambitious and insensitive, she constantly interferes with the lives of others by placing mercantile interests and middle-class conventions above human feelings and family loyalty. The second Grimes story, which begins eleven months after the death of the mother, focuses on Bedelia's concern for the future of the neglected family business. Her father's self-consuming grief, the subject of the final Grimes story, has convinced her that she must take some definite action to save the shop. She realizes that the "shop-boy," the timid Daniel, is the obvious choice to run the business, and that this can be accomplished through their marriage. Even though Alice, Liddy, and Tom, a weak-straw brother, are mentioned, this is Bedelia's story, marking her first step in taking control of the family shop and gaining dominance over the family's affairs. The differing reactions of Daniel and Bedelia to the dropping of the father's boot underline the complexity of the situation. For Daniel, the sound of the boot reminds him that Bedelia's father is still a barrier in their relationship. For Bedelia, the act sharpens her impression of Daniel's weak personality, while further intensifying her resolve to extract a commitment from him. There is little doubt that she will have her way at this fateful moment in the Grimes history and will become the controlling agent in the family's future.

In "Frail Vessel" the narrative draws a sharp contrast between Bedelia's formal arrangement with Daniel and Liddy's improbable romance with a solicitor, Alphonsus O'Brien. Within a year after their mother's funeral, both sisters are married. The central event, however, narrated within the third-person limited view of Bedelia's commonsense mind, is the collapse of Liddy's marriage because of Alphonsus's foolishness and Bedelia's insensitive reaction to Liddy's troubles. Having resented the intrusion of Liddy's frivolous and sentimental affair during her marital arrangements, Bedelia feels fully justified in her harsh treatment of Liddy, the "frail vessel" of the story. Her vengeful triumph, however, backfires on Bedelia. Her desire to have Liddy at home during her pregnancy is defeated by the discovery that Liddy, too, is pregnant. Significantly, Bedelia, whose marriage has been a practical but not an emotional success, also recognizes that Liddy, who faces the loss of her husband, still loves Alphonsus. On the surface, Bedelia's life prospers as she controls and manipulates the material and moral fate of the Grimes family; but her own harsh, practical mind denies her the chance to experience the happiness that sustains Liddy in her moment of loss.

In "The Little Prince," the Grimes saga shifts to the relationship between Bedelia and Tom, but the narrative still stresses the destructive effect of Bedelia's insensitive and calculating mind on the emotional history of the Grimes family. The first part of the story actually takes place between the events of "An Old Boot" and "Frail Vessel." Bedelia now has her understanding with Daniel, but she fears that Tom's carefree habits will destroy her plans for the family shop. By ignoring her feelings for her brother, she acts upon

the practicalities of the situation and convinces Tom that the only
place for the family's "black sheep" is America. The success of her
plan clears the way for her control of the family's fortunes, but the
price she pays is the loss of her brother's affection. During Bedelia's
fateful conversation with her brother, the light from a heart-shaped
vent shines upon Tom's face. After he leaves, however, the "little
patch of golden light, in the shape of a heart" (p. 211) falls upon a
blank wall.

The second part of "The Little Prince" is a chronicle of Bedelia's
marriage and the family shop, both of which are judged by the standard of Tom's growing financial share of the business. Daniel
realizes that their marriage, rather than being inspired by affection,
was conceived out of connivance. Bedelia's constant secretiveness
and her obsession with the money placed in the bank each month
for her brother convinces him that his wife is a born schemer. The
business, in spite of Bedelia's manipulations, never brings the
success to match her ruthless ambition. Thus, while the shop grows
smaller and smaller in value, the money takes on increasing importance as justification for the decisions which have isolated her from
the family.

During the first few years after Tom's departure, Bedelia receives
some information on Tom's whereabouts through the contrivance of
an accidental meeting between Tom and a former servant who had
emigrated to Boston. The contrived coincidence is stretched beyond
the point of credibility when twenty-seven years later the daughter
of the former servant decides to investigate Tom's disappearance
and finds someone she suspects is Bedelia's brother in a hospice for
the dying. This structural weakness, which resembles the flaws of
the novels, does not, however, lessen the devastating climax of "The
Little Prince." Bedelia's decision to see her dying brother in
America becomes far more than the apparent effort to gain legal
control over her brother's money. Now obsessed with the youthful
image of Tom as "the little prince," she seems determined to
restore the emotional bond between herself and her brother that existed before she sacrificed her brother's affection for control of the
family's shop. Even her brother's death fails to disturb Bedelia's il-
lusion, which eventually approaches a visionary experience: "For
the first time since she was a child, there was no connivance in
Bedelia's heart. All considerations of money had faded from her
mind. It was as if an angel of light had come and sat down beside
her in the dark cab, illuminating everything with a blinding

radiance" (p. 249). Her fate, however, is to pay heavily for her past actions. She discovers that she cannot recognize the dead man's face: "if it was her brother, something sundered them, something had severed the bonds of blood, and she knew him not" (p. 251). The harsh manipulations that have isolated Bedelia from her family cannot be undone or reversed. Bedelia's final numbness is a just punishment for a woman who has lived with connivance so long that even with "all connivance dead" her heart is "too old and cracked a vessel to hold any emotion at all, however precious, however small a drop" (p. 252).

"Loving Memory," published in *The Great Wave*, is the final Grimes story. On the surface, however, it seems strangely out of place in chronology and theme. The narrative events place it at the very beginning of the Grimes history, and the characters so prominant in the earlier stories fade completely into the background. Only Alice has an individual identity, while Bedelia, Tom, and Liddy become nothing more than the indistinguishable voices of the Grimes children. "Loving Memory" belongs to the parents, Mathias and Alicia, and the passionate and devoted love which haunts Mathias after Alicia's death, and develops into a mad obsession with the upkeep of her grave. Thematically, the love relationship between the parents and Mathias's unwillingness to accept Alicia's death seem to function as little more than a counterpoint to the emotional failures of the children. They fail to sustain any affection for each other or to find the same lasting love that united the parents.

As the final Grimes story, however, "Loving Memory" is a well-conceived part of Mary Lavin's master plan. The narrative flow of Mathias's early life, his brief courtship with Alicia, and their marriage, moves relentlessly to Alicia's death, the major emotional event in the Grimes history and the key to "A Visit to the Cemetery." Thus the general structure of the Grimes narratives is circular, the last story shaping and completing the circle by returning to the material of the first story. The theme of "Loving Memory" also completes the major thematic interests in the Grimes history. Rather than offering a sharply contrasting view of love and marriage, it illuminates the true cause of Bedelia's cruelty, Alice and Liddy's desperation, and Tom's pride. The love shared by the parents is so excessively self-centered that it isolates the children from the natural intimacy of family affection: "Love didn't thunder like a cataract down their staircase. It was all kept stored in their mother's room, and only their father had the key."[12]

Their parents' love is so exclusive that the children never have a chance to share in the happiness. Their father, once deprived of that love, cannot turn to his children for compensation, and ends his days by keeping a bizarre vigilance at his wife's grave. The figure to blame for the emotional deprivation of the Grimes family, however, is not the father. In "Loving Memory," it is the mother, the "poor bird" who "never made her nest in the heart of her children," who is the root cause for the tragic events that shape the Grimes history.[13] Though undeniably genuine and devoted, Alicia's love for Mathias fails to extend beyond its own self-consuming interest and becomes to those who observe it, yet are excluded from its magic, something secretive and monstrous.

The full impact of Alicia's influence can be properly understood only through a reading of the entire Grimes history. The terrible fact that the ghost of Alicia Grimes is the "Mad Mary" other mothers use to frighten their children home from the cemetery adds more than a bizarre twist to the ending of the last Grimes story. It focuses once more on those future events of the Grimes family already known, and reveals in a remarkable way that the failures of Bedelia, Liddy, and Tom are not a necessary outgrowth of middle-class conventions but the inevitable fate of those who do not share in the emotional life of others. The content of the Grimes stories is the Irish middle class, but Mary Lavin's basic theme is the failure of the human heart. The last lines of "Loving Memory," chanted by a mother who wants her children home, are a chilling reminder of the truth that awaits those who are denied love: " 'Have you forgotten Alicia Grimes? Oh-ho, you haven't! Alicia Grimes will get you! Alicia Grimes will get you!' "[14]

CHAPTER 5

The Later Fiction:
The Widow Stories

I N the 1960s and 1970s, Mary Lavin gradually moved away
from the story with a pattern and returned to the impressionistic
story that attempts to capture the emotional experience of her
character. She also added new strength to her fiction by objectifying
her painful adjustment to widowhood in a series of powerful portraits of widows. Several of her widow stories form a sequential
pattern of events in the life of middle-aged women struggling to
find their self-identity after the loss of their husbands. During this
period, Mary Lavin also created Vera Traske, her most
autobiographical character. After appearing in several stories of
emotionally isolated women, Vera finally emerges as the
autobiographical heroine in "Happiness." In this central story, Vera
expresses a philosophy which enables her to endure terrible suffering and still keep faith with herself and her work. "Happiness" is a
counterpoint to Mary Lavin's compelling studies of the great
loneliness of individuals trapped by their own emotional failures;
and Vera is one of her rare characters to recognize that life, with all
its tragic potential, also offers the chance for love, understanding,
and happiness.

I The Great Wave and Other Stories

Biographically, *The Great Wave* marks the beginning of a period
of recovery and achievement for Mary Lavin. The stories were
written during the time she was making a slow and painful effort to
recover from William Walsh's death. Several of the stories had been
published in the *New Yorker*, whose interest in her work had helped
her career. There is no strong indication, however, of any new
direction in *The Great Wave*. In fact, the collection offers the most

100

diverse group of stories in the Lavin canon. It has stories of human conflict, stories with a pattern, and stories with a strong Irish flavor.

"The Great Wave," the opening story in the collection, and "Bridal Sheets" are partly derived from a strange and beautful story that appeared in *Tales from Bective Bridge*. "The Green Grave and the Black Grave," the first Lavin story published in America, makes use of the same rhythms and idioms that J. M. Synge had borrowed from the primitive people of the Aran Islands. The story greatly resembles Synge's *Riders to the Sea* with its emphasis upon the fatalistic nature of the sea and the mythmaking character of the Irish people. Narrated in a bold but simple poetic style, "The Green Grave and the Black Grave" slowly reveals the tragic fate of a beautiful inland woman who marries a young man from the islands and tries desperately to match her power of love against the indifferent power of the sea. Since the fate of the young lovers has already been determined, but not yet revealed, at the beginning of the story, the role of the central characters, Tadg Mor and Tadg Beag, is choral. The function of their rituallike actions and dialogues, which reinforce the narrative tone, is to discover the profound nature of the tragedy of Eamon Og Murnan and his one-year wife.

At first, because they find the drowned body of Eamon Og floating at sea, Tadg Mor and Tadg Beag believe that Bean Og Eamon, though she will suffer greatly, has cheated the sea and its green grave and has won the return of her husband to the black grave. They learn, however, that Bean Og Eamon, determined not to be separated from her husband in life or death, was in the boat and has also drowned at sea. It appears that the sea, acting as an all-powerful and vengeful agent of fate, has claimed a terrible victory over the inland woman who dared challenge nature with the power of her love. Yet when Tadg Mor and Tadg Beag return from the cottages, they discover that the sea has taken back the body of Eamon Og from its resting place on the shore. In an ending that strongly suggests the mysterious and the supernatural, the sea, now acting as an instrument of the higher power of love, reunites the dead lovers:

The men of the island were caught down in the sea by the tight weeds of the sea. They were held in the tendrils of the sea anemone and the pricks of the sallowthorn, by the green sea-grasses and the green sea-reeds and the winding stems of the green sea-daffodils. But Eamon Og Murnan would be held fast in the white sea-arms of his one-year wife, who came from the inlands where women have no knowledge of the sea and have only a knowledge of love. (pp. 52 - 53)

"The Great Wave" lacks the poetic narrative of "The Green Grave and the Black Grave." Because it stresses a Christian view of the supernatural powers of the sea, it also lacks some of the primitive power of the earlier story. Yet "The Great Wave" resembles "The Green Grave and the Black Grave" in its use of island dialect and its emphasis upon the influence that the sea has on the simple lives of the islanders. It also shows traces of Synge's plays in its portrayal of Jimeen's mother and the handsome and daring Seoineen. Maurya, Seoineen's mother, actually bears the name of the tragic figure in *Riders of the Sea;* but it is Jimeen's mother, because she has lost her husband to the sea and refuses to allow her only son to go out in a currach, who shares Maurya's great knowledge and fear of the terrible power of the sea. Seoineen, even though he is a seminary student, is unmistakably modeled after the irrepressible hero of *The Playboy of the Western World:* "When Seoineen was a young fellow, he used to be the wildest lad on the island, always winning the ass-race on the shore, the first to be seen flashing into sight around the Point, and he coming up the straight, keeping the lead easily to finish at the pierhead."[1]

While Seoineen wins the approval of the islanders as their hero of the world, his good friend Jimeen is treated as a coward because his mother is so overprotective. The role of the sea, however, is to change the lives of Seoineen and Jimeen. With one great wave, every islander is drowned except the two friends. When Seoineen realizes the magnitude of the tragedy, he becomes so bitter that he turns away from his faith. Jimeen's reaction, however, is just the opposite. Out of his grief, he discovers a great mission in life. "The Great Wave" opens with Jimeen, now a bishop, being rowed to the island for one of his rare visits. From his perspective and out of his memories, the narrative retraces the island's tragedy and its effect on the only two survivors. After the story within a story, Jimeen, once again in his present role as bishop, remembers that he has not seen Seoineen since the terrible day. Out of his inquiries, however, he has learned that his childhood friend has become a bit odd. As the bishop leaves the island, one lonely figure, separated from the crowd of well-wishers, watches the boat from the island's highest point, the only spot untouched by the great wave and the haven that saved Seoineen and Jimeen from death. From the promontory, the perspectives of past and present merge into a momentary vision of one man reverently remembering the incredible turning point in his life, while another, sharing the same memories, looks on in embittered silence.

"Bridal Sheets" repeats some of the patterns of "The Green Grave and the Black Grave" and "The Great Wave." The story, relying heavily upon Peigin's island dialect for its particular character, stresses, once again, the sea as a terrible instrument of fate. The narrative of "Bridal Sheets" lacks the poetic style of "The Green Grave and the Black Grave," but the story stands as a strange and interesting companion piece to Mary Lavin's early tragedy of the islands. In "Bridal Sheets" the figures of Eamon Og and his one-year wife, who now is named Brede, return to act out their fates. In this version of the tragic marriage of an island man and an inland woman, however, Eamon Og has drowned and his body has been recovered. His wife, rather than sharing his fate, is preparing his body for burial. Together, the two stories function like the double ending of "The Widow's Son." In this second version of "The Green Grave and the Black Grave," the reader has the chance to see the terrible effect of Eamon Og's drowning on his one-year wife if she had survived his death. The narrative of "Bridal Sheets," lacking the poetic and choral tone of the earlier story, treats Brede's grief from a realistic and occasionally comic point of view. The women of the island, represented by Peigin, fail to understand why Brede is not reconciled to her husband's death, particularly since his body has been recovered from the sea. What Peigin learns is that Brede grieves because she never had the chance to wear any of her finery for her husband. Peigin, then, tries to ease Brede's suffering by suggesting that Eamon Og be buried in the linen bridal sheets that were never used. When she returns to Brede's cottage, however, she discovers Eamon Og's widow replacing the linen sheets with the old yellow sheets of their marriage bed. In this one instinctive act, the complexity of Brede's grief, her passion for her husband, her bitterness toward her island life, and her loyalty to her inland breeding, shines forth for one moment before fading into emotional numbness.

Among the variety of stories collected in *The Great Wave*, which also includes "Loving Memory," the last Grimes story, and the autobiographical "Lemonade," are several stories with a pattern. "Second Hand" relies upon a surprise ending for its narrative effectiveness. The story begins as an interesting study of two sisters, one

practical-minded, the other a dreamer, and their different reactions
to their mother's death. Their feelings are reflected in their disagreement over a pile of second-hand clothes. Essy feels nostalgic
about the old clothes, and wants to keep them. She gives in,
however, to the strong will of Mae, the older sister, who wants to
sell the clothes and use the money to fix up the house for lodgers.
Unfortunately, Charlie Mack, the hired man doing the wall-
papering, leaves his gaberdine on the pile of old clothes, and when
the sisters sell them they unwittingly include his coat. Whatever
small amount they get does not even match the money they now
owe Charlie for a new coat. The difference in outlook between the
sisters is intensified by the small tragedy of the gaberdine, but the
incident draws attention away from the emotional conflict in the
story to the irony of the sisters' impossible situation.

"My Molly" suffers not so much from a clever ending as it does
from an improbable one. The story depends for its success largely
upon the credibility of the title character and her relationship with
Sam, the village tanner. The premise for the concusion of "My
Molly" is that Sam, who has a way of disappearing from the village,
has done it again, and that several members of the village are either
asked or volunteer to find him in Dublin. Once the plot is established, Molly, after spending her time in Dublin shopping rather
than searching, wanders to the end of a pier, no disappointed bridge
in this story, and finds Sam standing there with nothing on but his
shirt. Once Molly restores his dignity, she learns that Sam's problem
is his great fear of someday dying alone. Ignoring Sam's queerness,
Molly solves everything by bringing Sam back to the village and
giving him a room in her house. Improbability aside, "My Molly"
ends on a happy, sentimental note in keeping with the generally
light tone of the story. "My Molly" neither challenges nor disturbs
but it is well intended and entertaining.

"The Yellow Beret" begins promisingly, but ends up as one of
the most glaring examples of a story with a pattern in the Lavin
canon. Based upon the actual newspaper account of two brutal
Dublin murders, the story narrates the surprising emotional and
moral effect of the murders on Don, Meg, and their son, Donny.
Don and Meg's heated discussion of the newspaper story at the
breakfast table exposes their underlying differences of personality
and outlook. Practical-minded and interested in details, Don sympathizes with the attractive seventeen-year-old girl slain at
dockside. Meg, who dreads even a vicarious experience with the

terrors of the outside world, identifies with the elderly spinster from
Sandford Road found murdered on the same night. Though their
disagreement concerns Meg's insistence that there is a connection
between the murders, the real issue is the opposed sensibilities of
husband and wife.

When they discover that Donny, a university student, has gone
out during the night and has not returned, Don and Meg are united
for the moment in their mutual concern for their son. Not surprisingly, one of their fears is that his disappearance is connected
with the murders of the previous night. Meg, after voicing the fear
and antagonizing her husband again, tries to explain that her
thoughts have nothing to do with her son: " 'It's as if all the
badness of the world, all the badness in *oneself*, rushes into one's
mind, and starts up a terrible reasonless fear. I *know* Donny is a
good boy' " (p. 186). When they see Donny walking on the road to
their house, Don and Meg recover their perspective on his disappearance.

Up to this point, "The Yellow Beret" resembles "A Tragedy" in
the way in which Mary Lavin uses a sensational external event as a
way of probing into the buried emotional life of a married couple.
When Donny tells his parents that he was worried about his ex-
aminations and decided to take a long walk, the narrative seems to
have reached the same objective as that in "A Tragedy." By arguing about the murders and involving their son's disappearance in
their dispute, Don and Meg resolve nothing. They do, however,
briefly expose the sharp differences in perspective and feeling
which normally remain under the surface.

Unfortunately, "The Yellow Beret" is destined to be a story with
a pattern. One of the missing clues in the investigation of the
spinster's murder is her yellow beret. Incredibly, Donny, after
developing a blister on his heel, found a yellow beret somewhere
near Sandford Road, and used part of it as a bandage. When Don
and Meg see "the bit of sweat-stained, blood-soaked yellow felt" (p.
191) all their previous fears return and take on a new reality. Realizing the dangers if his son goes to the police, Don suggests they
forget about the whole business and eliminate any possible
problem. Meg, however, believes that her son should tell the truth
and possibly help the police in their investigation. Their different
reactions to this real rather than imaginary crisis define even more
clearly their opposed sensibilities. Meg's sense of moral responsibility clashes sharply with Don's practical expediency. Finally, when

Donny agrees with his father, he exposes the fact that Meg has no
real emotional relationship with either her husband or her son. Unfortunately, the impact of this last insight into Meg's isolation is
marred by the intrusiveness of the yellow beret in shaping the crisis.
In many of her stories, Mary Lavin uses one striking symbol as the
focal point for the loneliness or bitterness of her main character. In
stories like "Second Hand" and "The Yellow Beret," however, the
symbol also functions as an artificial means to resolve the plot.
Because this type of story emphasizes its narrative cleverness rather
than its insight into the underlying truth of a character's lonely existence, the final result is often an entertaining but less interesting
study of human nature than her stories without an intrusive pattern.

"The Living," Mary Lavin's first contribution to the *New Yorker*,
adds another measure of diversity to *The Great Wave*. Occasionally,
in some of her earlier collections, she included a story about the intimate world of children. "Say Could That Lad Be I?," "The Bunch
of Grape," and "The Sand Castle," all observe the small joys and
sorrows of childhood. Though the conception of her children stories
ranges from the realistic to the allegorical, Mary Lavin is careful to
write each story from the limited perspective of the child's world. In
A Likely Story and *The Second Best Children in the World*, she expanded her interest in children into book-length, illustrated portraits of the special and magical world of the child's imagination.

"The Living" goes beyond her other children stories by focusing
on the way in which the child's experience draws him closer to the
pains and fears experienced by adults. Told from the first-person
point of view, the narrative, like that in Henry James's *What Maisie
Knew* and the opening stories in *Dubliners*, gains its objectivity
from the innocence of the child. He observes, but only vaguely
comprehends, a complex part of the adult world. At first, the plot of
"The Living" moves along at a light and comic pace. The narrator,
goaded by his more experienced friend, accepts the challenge to see
his first corpse. Knowing that the retarded son of a village woman
has just died, they decide to visit the cottage. Their hope of seeing
the body is fulfilled; but when they are invited by the grief-stricken
mother to stroke the hand of the corpse, the narrator's friend bolts
for the door. The narrator, however, is fascinated by his first encounter with death. Moreover, when he returns home, he senses a
new dimension in the teasing love-play between his mother and
father. He has a fleeting glimpse into the way in which his parents'
awareness of their own mortality haunts and intensifies their love

for each other. Intuitively, he grasps the terrible meaning behind the words, the living and the dead. No Gabriel Conroy, the narrator is still a child, and his world is still the living rather than the dead—at least for a little while longer.

Thematically and technically, the three most important stories in *The Great Wave* are "What's Wrong with Aubretia?," "The Mouse," and "In a Café." The first story contains an interesting variation on Mary Lavin's theme of emotional conflict, while the latter two, particularly "In a Café," anticipate the new direction in the stories of *In the Middle of the Fields.* "What's Wrong with Aubretia?" observes the emotional turmoil of a couple trying to overcome differences in class and temperament. Vera represents the declining authority and influence of the Irish upper class; but it is Alan, with his working-class background, who has trouble coping with their class differences. The more practical-minded of the two, Alan decides to take a job abroad and start a new life with Vera away from the constant reminders of their social and cultural differences. Unfortunately, Vera, romantic and fatalistic by nature, is not able to respond in an equally reasonable manner. She is caught between her love for Alan and her loyalty to her father. When faced with Alan's decision, she hesitates, exposing their real difference in sensibility. Not hampered by his emotions, Alan acts in a practical way. Vera, however, finds it impossible emotionally to accept his decision.

The basic strategy of "What's Wrong with Aubretia?" is the same as the earlier stories of opposed sensibilities. The third-person point of view, except for an occasional outside comment, is limited to the impressions of one character. Since the character selected is usually the more sensitive of the two, the obvious choice in "What's Wrong with Aubretia?" is the emotionally torn Vera. As in the final scene of "Sunday Brings Sunday," this impressionistic technique can reveal the inner reality of a character when her feelings become so intense that they dramatically alter external reality. The closeness of this approach to stream-of-consciousness fiction is particularly evident in the concluding moments of "What's Wrong with Aubretia?" Vera's feeling of isolation is so strong that when she hears a distant train whistle she visualizes the train carrying Alan away from her: "and in the darkness she saw the train rocketing through the night, all lit up like an excursion train, its golden lights strung loosely together and swaying gently with the sway of the carriages" (p. 116). Once she recovers from her dizzying loss of perspective and realizes that no train can be seen from her house, Vera restores the narrative's objectivity by discovering that the wavering lights in the distance are from the surrounding villas of the working-class families. The return of narrative perspective fuses the internal and external conflicts that seem destined to separate Alan and Vera for the rest of their lives.

At first, "The Mouse" reads like another version of "The Convert." The relationship between Leila, Mina, and Arthur is the same as the one between Naida, Mamie, and Elgar. Both shy and sensitive, Leila and Arthur are drawn together by their similar natures. Although much coarser than Leila, Mina manages to become a part of their relationship, and by "playing the mouse" with Arthur, wins him from Leila. All that Mina does is to run her finger along Arthur's wrist to remind him of the way his mother used to tease him as a child. The physical contact, however, lures Arthur away from the spiritual Leila to the more aggressive and sensual Mina. Within a few days, Arthur and Mina surprise everyone in the town by eloping.

In "The Convert" the key narrative event is the death of Naida Paston. It acts as a catalyst upon Elgar, intensifying his memories of his courtship with Naida and his awareness of his bitter marriage with Mamie. In "The Mouse" the narrative is completely detached from Leila, Mina, and Arthur. The story is told from the first-person point of view of a character who receives her information from her mother. Unlike the tragic Naida, Leila survives her jilting and lives a long life eased somewhat by her companionship with her close friend, the narrator's mother. Not only is Leila's survival a major difference between the plots of "The Convert" and "The Mouse," it also adds a new dimension to the latter story by allowing the narrative to explore the function of memory. Leila's memories of her romance with Arthur sustain her through her great loneliness. Her opportunity to tell her old friend the story of the mouse not only renews the past, it reaffirms the value of her memories: " 'She said she sometimes found herself doubting that there had ever been anything between them. She began to wonder if she had only invented the things he said, just to fill up the terrible vacancy in her heart' " (p. 34). Even though the narrator's mother does not fully understand or share the value of Leila's memories of Arthur, she helps reinforce the notion of memory as life's compensation for great suffering and loneliness. The narrator has to remind her mother, now a widow, that remembering is like talking about the dead: " '—you said it yourself about Father!—they are only really dead when they are no longer remembered by the living—' " (p. 32).

The influence of the dead upon the living is a constant theme in Mary Lavin's fiction. Several critics have commented on the near obsession with death that emerges from her stories. Zack Bowen, for example, claims that she "is preoccupied with death, and the effect of death upon the living is perhaps the most frequent motif in her writing."[2] The influence of memory is also a major factor in her writing. The basic narrative strategy in many of her stories is to tell the story retrospectively. She learned from Turgenev and Jane Austen that this approach breaks up the monotony of storytelling by balancing past and present as well as character and event. The significance of the close tie between death and memory in "The Mouse," however, is that it foreshadows the major concern of the type of story that dominates the next collection. In the early stories, death acts as a catalyst, revealing the truth about a character's life. In the widow stories, death becomes a presence, influencing a character's every action and thought. Memory, rather than functioning as a storytelling strategy, plays a vital role in the widow's adjustment to her new life.

This new and more complex treatment of memory and death is the key change in Mary Lavin's stories about widows. "Bridal Sheets" and "The Mouse" have widows who play significant roles in the outcome of the plots, but both stories retain the basic patterns and characteristics of her earlier fiction. "In a Café" is the only story in *The Great Wave* that clearly belongs to a new period in Mary Lavin's career. Because Mary Lavin gave her own first name to the central character, the story of a widow's painful and desperate effort to adjust to her husband's death also has a personal relevance. This fictional Mary, like her creator, lives on a farm in County Meath and has the worry of raising her young children on her own.

Even though Richard, her husband, has been dead for two years, Mary still struggles with the problem of beginning an active and independent life. She needs something "to give her back a semblance of the identity she lost willingly in marriage, but lost doubly, and unwillingly in widowhood" (p. 50). After two years, she still has difficulty forming an opinion or taking an action independent of what Richard would have said or done. Complicating her identity crisis, yet inextricably linked to it, is Mary's fear that the love and joy of

her past life with Richard will not sustain her in her effort to create
a new life. She remembers a part of his body—a hand, an arm, even
a foot—but she cannot recall the image of his face. Not only does
she have to undergo the painful adjustments of her present life and
the uncertainties of the future, she has to question the efficacy of
the past as a guiding force in her life: "And if she could not
remember him, at will, what meaning had time at all? What use
was it to have lived the past, if behind us it fell away so sheer?"
(p. 53).

The plot takes place in a small Dublin café frequented by artists.
Mary has arranged to have coffee there with Maudie, a younger
woman, recently a widow herself. Though they share a common understanding of the ordeals of widowhood, Mary is aware of the
marked differences between them. Faced with Maudie's youth and
beauty, she realizes that her friend's life, even with its tragedy,
faces outward into the future: "Why, right now, she was so fresh
and—looking at her there was no other word for it—virginal!" (p.
58). Her resentment of Maudie's advantages intensifies her feelings
of loneliness and insecurity. When she begins a conversation with
Johann van Stiegler, a foreigner who teaches art at one of the
colleges, she is drawn toward him. because of his isolation.
Recognizing in van Stiegler's invitation to his flat her own desperate
loneliness, Mary turns instinctively away from her shallow alliance
with Maudie to the deep feeling she senses van Stiegler shares with
her. After she leaves Maudie's company, she decides to visit the artist's flat and "the young man who was so vulnerable in his vanity:
the legitimate vanity of his art" (p. 65).

On the surface, "In a Café" ends in failure for Mary. At first
deceiving herself that her intentions are aesthetic, Mary finally admits to herself that she has come to the flat because of her
loneliness. At the last moment, she returns to the street. Her abortive effort at reaching out for some contact with human intimacy,
however, does have a dramatic effect upon her. Knowing that it is
Richard that she wants, her muffled cry to him stirs a vision in her
mind of her husband. For the first time in two years, she sees the
mental image of his face. When she goes to her car on the driver's
side, she senses that out of this frustrating episode, she has "got
back her rights" (p. 70). By facing the truth of her needs and fears,
Mary reclaims her own identity—and because she can now accept
Richard's death as a part of her past, she will have no trouble
remembering him in the future.

No story with a pattern, "In a Café" is told from a third-person limited point of view that intimately reflects Mary's emotional struggle. There are a few technical flaws in the narrative, like the Them-Her sequence, but the story still manages to capture the experience of Mary's emotional drama. The desired effect is for the reader to share in the experience of widowhood and the emotional problems Mary faces in living without her husband. At the end of the story, the narrative offers no easy solution or surprise ending. Instead, the reader has the opportunity to observe and experience the relationship between death and memory as Mary rediscovers her self-identity: "It was not a subject for amazement. By what means exactly had she got them back though—in that little café? That was the wonder" (p. 70).

II   In the Middle of the Fields
and Other Stories

The powerful theme of "In a Café" foreshadows the major interest in the next collection of stories. While all but one of the stories treat the general theme of love, the title story of *In the Middle of the Fields* and two others, "Heart of Gold" and "The Cuckoo-spit," explore the problems of widowhood. It is possible to read "In the Middle of the Fields" as a sequel to "In a Café." The widow in the story is nameless—but her dead husband's name is Richard, and she lives on a farm with her young children in County Meath. Considered chronologically, the emotional drama of "In the Middle of the Fields" occurs before "In the Café." Because the widow's fear of being alone is so intense in the former story, the death of the husband seems to have happened more recently than the two years that have elapsed in the latter. And there is no indication that the nameless widow has reached the point where she has recovered her sense of self-identity.

The plot of "In the Middle of the Fields" is simple enough. A lonely widow hires a neighbor to top her grass. On the night before mowing day, he comes to her cottage and unsuccessfully tries to delay the job. Before he leaves, however, he makes a fumbling attempt to kiss her. She wards off his advances, and sends him home to the care of his own wife. The complexity of the story is again created by the narrative method, which gives the reader the opportunity to share in the underlying emotional drama of the widow. The opening lines establish the widow's perspective as the point of view and stress her intense loneliness: "They thought she hugged tight every memory she had of him. What did they know about memory? What was it but another name for dry love and barren longing?"[3] Her futile longing for her dead husband is symbolized by her life at the farm, which like "a rock in the sea" is "islanded by fields" (p. 9). She is so sensitive to her isolation that she is afraid of being alone at night. She makes sure that each evening she is up-stairs in her room before it gets dark, and more than anything else, she dreads a knock at the door.

The narrative takes on another emotional dimension when the widow learns that Bartley Crossen, the man she has hired for the grass, has been married twice. She is told the story of his happy marriage to Bridie Logan, a wild and romantic spirit, and its tragic end. Bridie, shortly after the birth of her son, leaped upon a bicycle in an impulsive moment and rode it until she hemorrhaged. After his wife's death, Bartley, according to his neighbor, eventually forgot his first wife and married a good woman who raised his son. Though struck by the tragedy of Bartley's first marriage, the widow is more interested in his emotional transition to the second. She identifies her own married life with his blissful marriage, and can-not believe that Bartley was able to forget his first wife. Told that when the tree falls the shadow no longer stands, she still wonders if he ever really forgot her.

Her answer literally comes knocking at her door when Bartley turns up that night to get out of his commitment to cut the grass. He is so taken by her isolation and girlish vulnerability that he tries unsuccessfully to kiss her. Once rejected, he bursts into tears and tells her the rest of the story. The widow learns that Bartley married Mona, his second wife, because she took care of his son during the difficult period after Bridie's death. Learning that circumstance rather than love led to his second marriage, the widow now un-derstands the truth about Bartley's marriages and why he has acted so foolishly. Realizing that he never forgot his first wife, she tells him that Bridie is responsible for his indiscretion: " 'You thought you could forget her . . . but see what she did to you when she got the chance!' "(p. 27). Her strategy has the immediate effect of get-ting rid of her unwelcome visitor, but it also reaffirms in her own mind what she had come to doubt—that her memories of Richard, inextricably bound up with feelings of dry love and barren longing, will stay with her and haunt her in the future.

"Heart of Gold" is different in several ways from the other stories treating the theme of widowhood. The heart of gold in this story belongs to a widower rather than a widow; and, rather than suffering from any profound sense of loneliness, he is busy courting the woman he wanted to marry in the first place. The narrative view in "Heart of Gold" reflects the views of the spinster rather than the widower. Thus the past history of Sam and Lucy's abortive courtship is remembered sympathetically, while Sam's surprising engagement and marriage to Mona is presented unfavorably. Lucy emerges as a disappointed spinster, denied by a conniving shopgirl the chance to marry the only man she ever really wanted. When Sam returns from Dublin immediately after Mona's death and proposes to Lucy, it appears that her destiny has resumed its natural course after long years of bitter interruption: "on the day Mona died it seemed that she'd been given back, in an instant, her lost role. She was once more what she had been—a romantic figure, tantalizing, unpredictable" (p. 50).

Until Sam and Lucy are married, "Heart of Gold" is little more than a bittersweet story of two lovers separated by fate and their own timidity, but finally reunited in their autumn years. Once they board a train for Dublin, however, the story moves in the direction of "In a Café" and "In the Middle of the Fields." Lucy's first insight into the dramatic change in her life comes when she notices her family's indifference to the news of her marriage. She begins to realize that her marriage reduces her in their eyes from a romantic figure of intrigue to Sam's second wife. While sitting on the speeding train, she also notices that the influence of Sam's first wife increases as she moves closer and closer to her life in Dublin. Through Sam's incessant talk about Mona's generosity and selflessness, Lucy begins to feel that Mona not only blessed her marriage, she arranged it from her deathbed. When she guesses that Sam wants to visit Mona's grave as soon as they arrive in Dublin, she becomes so panic-stricken by the sudden knowledge of the influence the dead woman has over her life that she bolts from her chair. For a few desperate minutes, she tries to find a way out of her situation, until she finally accepts her role in the real world: "She was committed to being real at last. Sam had committed her. It was a long way back, but she'd have to go back to him" (p. 70). And a part of going back to Sam is accepting Sam's past with Mona as a part of her new life.

"The Cuckoo-spit" is not only the best of Mary Lavin's widow
stories, it is one of the finest that she has ever written, rivaling
"Sunday Brings Sunday" in its unity of form and content. "The
Cuckoo-spit" also forms a sequential pattern with "In a Café" and
"In the Middle of the Fields." Once again the widow's husband is
named Richard. While there is no mention of her having children,
she does live on a lonely farm in the middle of the fields. She also
remembers going through the emotional ordeals faced by her
counterparts: " 'You cannot imagine how awful it was in those first
months, having to listen to people talking about him, going on and
on about him—mostly his family, of course, but my own people
were nearly as bad, and friends and neighbors. Everybody. And all
the time they were getting him more and more out of focus for
me' " (p. 81).

The narrative of "The Cuckoo-spit" takes place four years after
the death of Richard, thus chronologically placing the story after
"In the Middle of the Fields" and "In a Café." Possibly because a
longer period of time has elapsed between the widow's present life
and the death of her husband, "The Cuckoo-spit" is a more
autobiographical study of widowhood than the other stories. The
narrator's description of the farm, for example, is similar to Mary
Lavin's personal sketches of the Abbey Farm in Bective. Of far
greater importance are the narrative details about the dead husband, Richard. His interest in politics, frustrated by his declining
health, and his strength of character are drawn directly from the
personality of William Walsh. Mary Lavin's selection of Vera
Traske for the name of her widow is also highly significant. She first
used Vera for the name of the romantic and fatalistic character in
'What's Wrong with Aubretia?" In "The Cuckoo-spit" the widow
has the same temperament as her namesake, and faces a similar loss
of companionship because of social and cultural barriers. What
Mary Lavin achieves in Vera Traske is the joining together of her
personal feelings and her most powerful theme into one character.
What emerges is the most autobiographical character in her fiction—one that appears several times in later collections.

The opening scene of "The Cuckoo-spit" is one of the most impressive in Mary Lavin's fiction. The narrative begins with a ghostly
evocation of the countryside surrounding the farm that reflects
Vera's shadowy existence since her husband's death. When a
strange young man steps forward out of the unreality of the night
and introduces himself only by the name of Fergus, the atmosphere
becomes mythic. Though quickly identifying himself as the nephew

of the neighbor who lives across the river, Fergus draws Vera into a disturbing conversation, challenging her to "no more turn aside and brood/Upon love's bitter mystery." The purpose of the timelessness of the opening scene, however, is not to set the stage for a ghost story like "The Dead Soldier" or some fable of the human heart. Instead Mary Lavin uses the opening scene to create an objective atmosphere for the story of a delicate and complex relationship which in itself has timeless overtones.

The May-September romance of Fergus and Vera has its own universal appeal because of the tragic potential in love's desperate race against indifferent time. Mary Lavin, however, reverses the traditional roles in the relationship and risks straining the credibility of her story. Her way of countering the danger is to work with two totally different perspectives from within the relationship itself. What she achieves in "The Cuckoo-spit" is a complex point of view reflecting different emotional levels and responses, while retaining the objectivity of the opening scene. Representing all the energy and promise of youth, Fergus sees their affair of the heart as improbable but not impossible. Sensing the passion and intimacy of Vera's past marriage, he tries to revive the emotional happiness Vera had with Richard. While she resists a new intimacy, he argues for the priority of love. Vera, on the other hand, sees the need for love as part of the dead past. Her view is that by accepting "life's defeats" she recognizes the reality of her age. When she hears Fergus arguing for the tradition of love, she mockingly agrees that she, too, has heard and read about such things: " 'Elderly housemaids jumping out of closets at little boys!' " (p. 93).

Following the strategy of so many of Mary Lavin's earlier stories, "The Cuckoo-spit" has one symbol that becomes the focal point for the emotional complexities of the relationship between Fergus and Vera. At the end of their second meeting, they come upon a neglected rosebush in front of the farmhouse. Fergus accepts one of the roses, only to find what he believes is a cuckoo-spit on it. His excitement is quickly dampened, however, when Vera tells him that the cuckoo never comes near a house. What they both discover is that the "cuckoo-spit" hides a plant louse living on the juice of the plant. When Vera flicks the white blob onto the back of her hand, she watches a pale sickly yellow aphid crawl out of it. Unnerved by the touch of the insect, Vera is equally disturbed by the touch of Fergus's hand upon hers as he wipes away the last traces of the secretion.

The immediate effect of the moment is to bring Vera and Fergus closer together. The touch of another's flesh, so long denied Vera, begins to lure her away from a passive acceptance of life's failures toward a renewed awareness of life's feast. For Fergus, the moment gives him the response he has wanted. He now senses an emotional bond between them. The moment, however, also hints at the dangers of their growing intimacy. The deceptive sign of summer counterpoints whatever promise each feels in their relationship. Their different reactions to the plant louse, coupled with the narrative implication that something sinister lurks under the appearance of beauty, actually foreshadow the impending failure of their affair.

The end of their intimacy comes as abruptly as its beginning. Their agreement to meet in Stephen's Green leads to a confrontation of desire and reality. More heroic than Prufrockian, Fergus forces the moment to a crisis in the hope of winning a total commitment. But Vera, recognizing the impossibility of overcoming their difference in age, resists her natural impulses. Though promising to let him stay the night with her, she drives back to her farm alone despite his boast that she will never be able to leave him. When they meet again nearly a year later the wisdom of Vera's decision is immediately apparent. Though they recapture the atmosphere of their old intimacy, the passion and vitality of their earlier encounter is gone. Vera's planned visit to Richard's grave also suggests that her place is more with the memories of her past life than with the youthful promise of a relationship with Fergus. By refusing to go with her to the cemetery, Fergus, by reaction more than thought, acknowledges that his future life will have no link with Vera's past. The more reflective of the pair, Vera tries to comfort Fergus with the thought that love sometimes has more to do with external influences than with people. Fergus, however, interrupts her homily to remind her of the joy of their brief love. Yielding to the unerring instincts of youth, Vera enriches rather than corrects his statement by reminding him of the pain as well.

The final good-bye of "The Cuckoo-spit," following Vera's farewell to Fergus, is an unspoken part of the narrative. It quietly announces the final separation of Fergus and Vera. What the ending of the story offers is a reflective atmosphere to weigh the emotional effect of the intense but unrealized love affair upon Fergus and Vera. With his instinctive sense of the joy of love and his new knowledge of its pain, Fergus is now emotionally prepared for the happiness and sorrow of a later relationship that will have the same potential for intimacy without the insurmountable physical barrier. Vera already knows the bitter pain of love, but Fergus's reminder of the joy gives back to her something of her emotional identity before her life with Richard. Each gains something from the relationship—still, no matter what the emotional compensation, the cruel fact remains that love in "The Cuckoo-spit" does not conquer all. Though the story opens with the evocation of a mysterious atmosphere, it ends with no magic kiss or potion, no divine reward for pure and selfless devotion that transforms the lovers' plight into a state of pure bliss. This modern inverted version of Beauty and the Beast is doomed to an unhappy ending because the barrier separating these enchanted lovers is the unrelenting and irreversible movement of time.

The three remaining stories of *In the Middle of the Fields* have nothing to do with the theme of widowhood. Each, however, offers a variation upon the general theme of isolation which plagues most of the relationships in Mary Lavin's fiction. "The Lucky Pair" is the story of a lukewarm courtship between a first-year law student and the auditor of the Student's Law Society. What makes them a lucky pair is their knowledge of another couple, secretly married, whose violent quarrels have led to a separation. Ironically, the safe and secure future life of the lucky pair pales in comparison to the passionate life of the married pair. Once again, a rational approach to love seems a sorry compromise even if the alternative is tragic. "The Lucky Pair" is a brief reminder that Mary Lavin sympathizes with those who face the dangers of love rather than those who prefer the sheltered security of a cautious and measured existence.

"One Summer" and "The Mock Auction," the last two stories of *In the Middle of the Fields*, represent Mary Lavin's successful return to the novella form. "One Summer," a carefully controlled study of love lost and never regained, has special significance in the Lavin canon. With only a few minor changes, it continues the story of Vera and Alan in "What's Wrong with Aubretia?" Alan's threatened emigration to Australia at the conclusion of "What's Wrong with Aubretia?" is now a reality in "One Summer." The narrative opens on a strong note of crisis. Alan has left by boat for Australia and Vera's father has suffered a stroke. Deeply affected by the simultaneity of Alan's departure and her father's serious illness, Vera feels responsible for both events. She fears that if her father dies she has lost Alan unnecessarily. It was his objection to Alan that led to their separation. Yet she also feels that the strain in the close relationship with her father, caused by her desire to see Alan against his wishes, led to his attack.

The only changes in the characterizations of Alan, Vera, and her father reshape the struggle between father and suitor into a country-city rather than class conflict. Mary Lavin accomplishes this by intensifying the intimacy between father and daughter and by changing the suitor's profession from an architect to a Dublin solicitor. By drawing upon her own relationship with Tom Lavin and by giving Alan the same profession as William Walsh, she also further personalizes a story that already has the autobiographical Vera in it. Her reason for continuing the drama of Alan and Vera is to capture the emotional ordeal of a different yet equally devastating form of isolation from that experienced in the widow stories. Not only does Vera have to live with her separation from Alan, she has to contend with the resentment and alienation now existing between her father and herself.

After Vera's ambivalent reaction to the news of her father's stroke, she turns away from thoughts about Alan to a new concern for her father's physical and emotional welfare. Immediately, some of the old intimacy returns to their relationship. In spite of what has happened recently, a new surge of love passes between them. What follows is a brief glimpse into Vera's past life with her father. She remembers the "miracles of love" he performed for her to compensate for the early death of her mother. As she grew up, she soon realized that her father was living for her. On one occasion, when she almost killed herself in a fall, her father graphically illustrated his emotional dependency by holding an empty revolver to his head and pulling the trigger as a warning of what he would do if something happened to her.

Over the years, Vera watched her father's attitude harden into a conviction that she would never marry. Once she met Alan, his conviction turned into an aggressive and hostile resistance. Her father, by imposing such a burden on their relationship, forced Alan to insist that Vera decide between the two. Determined to rid their relationship of her father's influence, he proposed a new life for them in Australia. Willing to marry Alan but unable to accept a long physical separation from her father, Vera decided to stay behind.

Whatever Vera's reasons for not leaving, she now faces the complex situation of nursing her dying father while she tries to contact Alan about the dramatic change in her affairs. Her efforts, however, are frustrated and finally defeated on both counts. She quickly discovers that she is losing her intimate place with her father to his nurse. Not only does she fail to reach Alan with her letters, she learns through his letters that he has formed a shipboard romance with a young woman "*so* like" Vera. All that remains for her is to keep her daily vigil while her father slowly loses touch with the living. Vera's reward for keeping faith with her father, however, is a brutal lesson for those who ignore or deny their chance for love. Her father's urgent questions about the meeting of loved ones in the next life lead to one last agonizing discovery. Assuring her father that there must be a hereafter or love would have no meaning, she assumes that he is thinking about her. Shockingly, she discovers that his deathbed vision is of her mother. Perhaps the loneliest of all of Mary Lavin's characters, Vera faces an empty life without any prospect for intimate human contact and without any pure memories of past intimacies. Unlike Mary Lavin's widows, Vera is totally isolated by time. Betrayed by the past and denied the future, she has no self-identity to fall back upon. Even in the hereafter she can count on no one to meet her—and, according to Vera herself, without that last hope life has no meaning at all.

The bitter reality of Vera's fate is a prelude to "The Mock Auction," one of Mary Lavin's starkest tales. The relationship between "One Summer" and "The Mock Auction," however, is not immediately apparent. If anything, the early narrative of the latter story resembles the pattern of another story, "The Small Bequest." Miss Lomas is another Miss Blodgett in occupation and dilemma. The housekeeper of Brook Farm, an outfarm of the Garrett estate, has an informal financial arrangement with her employers. Because they regard her as an indispensable part of the farm, she is given no wages. Instead she is told to take whatever money she needs from the household expenses. An ample, well-fed symbol of country prosperity and comfort, she is known by the local people as the Regent of Brook Farm.

The death of one of the Garrett brothers exposes the potential danger of Miss Lomas's position. Not being a blood relative of the Garretts, she is vulnerable to any abrupt change in the Garrett estate. When she learns Brook Farm was left intestate, she fears that the Garretts might lose the place. Assured that George, the remaining brother, will buy it back, she relaxes until she learns that there must be a public auction. Undaunted by the muddled legalities surrounding Brook Farm, George and Mr. Parr, his lawyer, arrange a

mock auction so that Christy, the family black sheep, can purchase
the property and keep it in the estate. The arrangement ends the
confusion for the moment, but Christy's surly presence on the farm
is a constant and unhappy reminder of the tenuous nature of Miss
Lomas's position. And when George suddenly drops dead less than
a year after his brother's death, Miss Lomas is caught once more in
a threatening web of circumstances.

Up until the death of George Garrett, the narrative of "The Mock
Auction" reveals a pattern of external events which completely
reverses the fortunes of Miss Lomas. If "The Mock Auction" had
ended at this point, it would have become another example of the
story with a pattern. Fortunately, however, the narrative relentlessly pursues Miss Lomas's fate beyond the cruel twists of fate.
Whatever the pattern of the first half of the story, the second half
emerges as an unyielding study of the bitter symbiotic relationship
between Miss Lomas and Christy. Both afraid of being driven off
Brook Farm, they form a strange alliance to defend their interests.
But while they put up a united front against the world, they act out
their mutual contempt for each other: "All that had happened was
that where he and she had previously been divided by hate, they
now were bound by it" (p. 187).

Once Miss Lomas and Christy settle into their new existence at
Brook Farm, they share the responsibility for its gradual collapse.
Their hatred manifests itself in the very deterioration of the property. What Miss Lomas quickly learns is that after her years of in-
dolent service as the Regent, she is ill-prepared for the practical
duties of housekeeping. Her cleaning efforts are either ineffectual
or harmful. She finally gives up scrubbing and washing because she
believes her work is hastening the disintegration of the house.
While Miss Lomas unwittingly contributes to the ruin of the interior of the house, Christy is busy raping the land for any immediate profit. Though he manages to buy food and pay the rates
and interest on the mortgage, his random plunder over the years of
everything of value outside and inside the house is devastating. By
the time he completes his ferreting and leaves Brook Farm, he has
completely decimated the property.

Incredibly, after being abandoned by Christy, Miss Lomas
decides to restore Brook Farm to its former health and prosperity.
Like a ghoulish vision of Scarlett O'Hara, she sets forth from her
ruined farmhouse in her ancient and slightly absurd costume to convince the lawyer Parr that Brook Farm can be saved. A ravished and

avenging figure from the past, she rises up before Mr. Parr to urge his supervision of the miraculous restoration she envisions in her mind: "Indeed she was overcome by such a rush of energy and enthusiasm it seemed that when she got back there she would turn out every room at Brook Farm and overtake in a few hours all she had failed to accomplish in a decade" (p. 204). Though exhausted by the effort, she convinces Mr. Parr to visit the property. Mr. Parr's reaction to the devastation of Brook Farm is predictable; but either out of pity for Miss Lomas or respect for the Garrett family, he decides to begin the repair work and at least "put a stop to the inroads of decay" (p. 214). Indomitably, Miss Lomas, in the hour of her greatest loneliness and despair, through madness, flattery, and ignorance rescues her beloved Brook Farm.

Miss Lomas's successful defiance of fate contrasts sharply with Vera's hopelessness at the end of "One Summer." Though each character is faced with the loss of everything of value, only Miss Lomas finds the inner strength to stand up to her ordeal. Her capacity to endure great hardship after a life of bliss is what sustains her through the long years with Christy. Unlike Vera, who fails to follow her instincts, Miss Lomas never loses her faith in Brook Farm during its terrible decay. Her final vision is a revelation of the power of faith and love to overcome the worst that life has to offer: "Brook Farm was cut out sharply in the full strength of its cutstone. It was, indeed, a little gem, and in spite of decay the concept of beauty that inspired it had outlived its execution in perishable form. As for the land—was not the earth at all times indestructible?" (p. 214).

The last story of *In the Middle of the Fields* makes the strongest statement about the human spirit's ability to endure great suffering and still keep faith with life. After the stories of widows struggling to overcome their great personal losses and of women failing to act upon their true feelings, "The Mock Auction" stands out as a tribute to the enduring strength of the human heart. Miss Lomas is the least likeliest of Mary Lavin's heroines to overcome personal misfortune; but her love for Brook Farm and her dedication to its way of life sustain her through the worst of times. In spite of the grim realities of "The Mock Auction," Miss Lomas's single act of determination counters the tragedy and despair of the earlier stories in the collection. It also symbolizes a philosophy that slowly emerges from *In the Middle of the Fields* to take definite shape in the opening story of her next collection.

III   Happiness and Other Stories

The title story of *Happiness* explores in greater depth the philosophy of "The Mock Auction." One of Mary Lavin's most personal stories, it also brings to a climax a growing tendency in her later fiction to use autobiographical materials. Not surprisingly, she turns to Vera once again for the story of a mother's legacy to her children. In "Happiness" there is little effort to disguise the autobiographical nature of the story. Like Mary Lavin, Vera has been forced to endure the early death of her husband, named Robert rather than Richard in this story. As in the case of William Walsh, Robert died at the beginning of a promising political career, leaving Vera with three young girls, one only a year old, to care for on her own. "Happiness" also has a thinly veiled portrait of Mary Lavin's father as well as a rare glimpse at the character of her mother. Once again her father is remembered as a wide and happy man, radiating his happiness in everything he did. In contrast, the mother is viewed as a temperamental and demanding woman, "a complicated mixture of valiance and defeat."[4] Dissatisfied with her marriage in spite of her husband's generosity of spirit, "Miss Imperious" has spent her life refusing to be shaken in her belief that disappointment is her lot in life. Her behavior adds one more burden to her daughter's life.

Vera takes on more autobiographical importance in "Happiness" than she does in any of the previous stories. A widow with the lonely responsibility of raising three young daughters, she also seems to share her creator's occupation. Though never directly stated in the narrative, Vera's professional interest in writing is implied in her frantic efforts to keep up with her paper work and her many correspondences. Though chaotic, her outside activities in the eyes of her family have a decidedly literary quality: "The chaos of her life was as personal as an act of creation—one might as well try to finish another person's poem" (pp. 25 - 26). Another new autobiographical dimension of Vera's life is her intimate relationship with Father Hugh, an obvious Michael Scott figure. There is no talk of Father Hugh ever leaving the priesthood to marry Vera—the children believe that he is trying to save her soul so that he can "be sure of her in the next world" (p. 11). But even the neighbors are scandalized by their personal intimacy. Indeed their warm companionship and their deep mutual concern for each other obviously reflect the relationship that had developed between

Mary Lavin and Michael Scott in the years leading up to their marriage.

Perhaps because of the closeness of her heroine to her own personality and interests, Mary Lavin uses the first-person point of view of one of the older daughters in "Happiness" rather than the voice of Vera herself. Through the loving yet occasionally skeptical voice of the daughter, the narrative summarizes Vera's early happiness and her later grief. Not only does it describe Vera's glowing relationship with her father and her frustrating life with her mother, it reveals her terrible sense of loss in the immediate years after Robert's death. The main purpose of the narrative, however, is to capture and evaluate Vera's philosophy of life. Though the girls hear their mother constantly talking about happiness, none of them really understands what Vera means by it. They are told never to confuse it with pleasure, or think sorrow its opposite. As to Father Hugh's solemn belief that sorrow is a necessary part of happiness, Vera, while recognizing some freakish truth in the notion, knows that its flaw is that some people substitute sorrow for happiness. Vera's own belief is that happiness can coexist with unpleasantness and terrible pain.

Fascinated by their mother's strange notion of happiness, the girls remain somewhat skeptical about ever defining or knowing it themselves. Occasionally, they also find it rather difficult to believe that their mother possesses the elusive quality of happiness, considering the emotional ordeals she has experienced. Vera, however, tells them that her father was a happy man even when in dreadful pain just before his death. The girls also learn that their grandmother was very unhappy. Impressed by this insight into the family's emotional history, they conclude that happiness might be a vague legacy even though it did not help their grandmother. They also learn from their mother that a person can feel happiness or its absence even if he does not understand it.

In spite of their confusion and doubts, all of the children sense that their mother has this mysterious happiness. They feel it when she talks about the delicate joys of her childhood and her life with their father. They still fail, however, to give a definite meaning to what she calls her happiness: "What was it, we used to ask ourselves—that quality that she, we felt sure, misnamed? Was it courage? Was it strength, health, or high spirits? Something you could not give or take—a conundrum? A game of catch-as-catch can?" (p. 16). One of the girls in frustration suggests it is a sham.

Only in the delirium of her mother's final hours does Bea, the most
skeptical of the girls, understand her mother's happiness. She
realizes that her mother's incoherent ramblings are fragments of
past thoughts and feelings from the time she tried to prevent
Robert's death by surrounding his hospital bed with freshly picked
daffodils. Understanding this and sharing in the emotion, Bea
quietly urges her mother to rest now that her struggle with life is
over. In the last moment of her life, Vera finally unloosens her hold
on happiness.

What Vera passes on to Bea is her feeling that life, no matter
what its pleasures or sorrows, is worth the struggle to live it fully.
Zack Bowen sees this feeling and Mary Lavin's own "history and
personality" as "an embrace of the joys and pains of life and an appreciation of their unique and memorable characteristics."[5] Even
though there are other Vera stories in the Lavin canon, it is significant that her autobiographical heroine dies in "Happiness." It underlines the importance of Vera's theory of happiness as a summary
of Mary Lavin's professional career and her private life. This elusive
quality of happiness reflects her own capacity to understand and
accept the often contradictory emotions and forces of life. Once this
is done, she reconciles them in a firm commitment to life no matter
what disappointments and difficulties tempt her to give in to
despair and defeat.

There is no pattern of autobiographical stories in *Happiness.*
Rather, the opening story stands out as a unique contribution to the
collection. What follows is a variety of stories that for the most part
repeat the general themes and patterns of her earlier fiction. The
weakest story, "The New Gardener," relies upon the formula of the
story with a pattern for its success. The first-person narrator tells
the tragic story of Clem, her new gardener, whose gentleness con-
tradicts the terrible truth she learns about him. A loving father and
wonderfully successful gardener, Clem delivers little homilies about
the value of all living things and their need for gentle care. As Clem
lectures softly on the need for kindness and love, however, the
narrator notices a few oddities that foreshadow an unusual and surprising ending. For one thing Clem's precious daughter, Pearl, has
a long sickle-shaped scar on the inside of her arm. And somehow
this scar seems linked to the fact that Clem hardly ever mentions
the mother of his children. Once Clem reacts violently to a lad stick-
ing a fishing hook into the tender part of a frog's body, the reason
for his mysterious behavior is only a detective or two away. As if

summoned by the cry of the frog (or the needs of this patterned story), the detectives appear out of nowhere to arrest Clem, while assuring him that his children will be well treated by the authorities. This childlike gardener, resembling Lenny in Steinbeck's *Of Mice and Men* in his gentleness and latent violence, is led away for the murder of his wife.

"One Evening" is another example of a *Dubliners*-type story of a youth's sudden encounter with the complex emotions of the adult world. Though the ending of the story is hardly Joycean, its narrative pattern is the same as the first three stories in *Dubliners*. Told from the limited perspective of a teen-age youth, "One Evening" contrasts Larry's budding romantic impulses and the knowledge he gains about the failed relationship of his parents. When he returns home after an awkward evening of courting, he discovers the house in total darkness and his father sitting alone in his car. Incapable of understanding the meaning of his father's cryptic words about killing his mother, Larry, after failing to convince his father to return to the house with him, finds his mother alone in the drawingroom. What she says to him also makes little sense to her son. She tells him that there are things he will have to know about his father, but all she reveals is how she played the piano during their courtship. Sensing that the truth is beyond his limited experience, Larry listens to his mother's rambling memory of a moment now emotionally dead for her. When she begins to play upon a moth-eaten piano a ghastly version of a tune she played for his father, Larry can no longer tolerate his mother's behavior. Not understanding what has happened between his parents, he does sense that they have exposed their emotional failure. Instinctively, he rebels against their emptiness, determined to seek out a life of his own in which love is not talked about in the past tense.

The ending of "One Evening" is more hopeful than those in Joyce's stories of youthful encounters with the corruption and frustration of the adult world. Larry's decision to leave his mother with her bankrupt memories and respond to the promise of the summer evening is a more positive assertion of youth than any of the gestures of escape in the opening stories in *Dubliners*. The basic emotional situation in "One Evening," however, is similar to the brief ordeals which suddenly confront Joyce's innocents. In each case a youth encounters emotional depths which taunt and defy his limited range of experience. Though incapable of understanding his predicament, he does feel the tension of the moment. He also senses that in some strange way the adult is trying to draw him into some private failure. Still the inexperienced youth, however, he escapes for the moment from any corruption, even though time itself will soon drive him into this ominous adult world for the rest of his life. In Joyce's stories, the atmosphere of paralysis is so pervasive that little hope exists for even his youthful Dubliners. In Mary Lavin's stories, the failure of love is equally pervasive; but the fact that it once existed holds out some tentative promise that love is still possible in a world better suited for pain and sorrow.

"A Pure Accident" is one of the few stories in the Lavin canon that has a priest as its main character. In an earlier story, "A Wet Day," the priest was portrayed by the agnostic narrator as a villainous human being. Father Patton's problem in "A Pure Accident" is more his twisted sense of humanity than his lack of humanity. The canon is a far better example of the selfish religious mind represented by Father Gogarty in "A Wet Day." The canon's stinginess and his insensitivity to the needs of his parishioners sets the stage for the pure accident of the story. Because he resents the fact that some poor villager has been stealing a few pennies from the poor box, he orders Father Patton to hide in the church and wait for the thief. Even though he knows that his assistant is not fit for the job because of his nervous condition, the canon still sends him to catch the penny thief. Unfortunately, his premonition that Father Patton will botch the job comes true. Instead of pouncing upon the thief, he knocks down a woman making a night visit to the church. What follows is a series of nightmarish events. Refusing to listen to Annie's cries of pain, Father Patton worries only about the canon. He forces her brother and his friends to drive Annie home; but by the time they finish carrying her from car to car they aggravate the original injury into a compound fracture of the hip.

While Annie recuperates in the hospital, she has two related worries, her large hospital bill and the fact that she has received no visit from Father Patton. Once she learns that she may have to pay the bill, she sends for him. When Father Patton turns up at the hospital, his reason for not coming sooner is painfully apparent. Distraught and irrational, he is so disturbed by the present situation that he confesses his emotional problems before becoming a priest. His frustration with his own personal failings and his bitterness toward the church authorities mount into a dangerous tirade against Annie and any nurse or hospital aide who comes near him. By the time he leaves the hospital, he has unknowingly exposed his repressed sexual feelings and his unnatural closeness with his mother. Emotionally ill, he wanders about looking for some immediate relief from feelings made even more torturous by the confinement of the priesthood:

> His life had been all boxes, he thought. First there was that box of a cubicle in the seminary. In it he was more awkward than most, being bigger boned than most. After that it was box after box; nothing but boxes: confessional boxes, poor boxes, collection boxes, and pamphlet boxes. Even God was kept in a box, shut up and locked into one. What was the Tabernacle but only a box. (p. 100)

Only the last thought shocks Father Patton back into some measure of self-control. This glimpse into his twisted emotions, however, reveals a violent inner world only hinted at in other stories. One of Mary Lavin's few studies of madness, "A Pure Accident" is made even more compelling by the close tie between the pressures of the priesthood and Father Patton's overwhelming sense of confinement. Rather than granting him some relief from his anxiety, the church only increases his burden. In *Mary O'Grady*, Larry, the youngest of Mary's sons, almost becomes a spoiled priest because his superiors are worried that his older brother's mental illness may be a sign that Larry is not strong enough to perform the demanding duties of a priest. "A Pure Accident" is an ironic fulfillment of that priestly prophecy. Indeed this poor servant of the Church is ill-suited for his profession—but the Church as an institution also fails because it seems to encourage insensitivity and niggardly behavior rather than loving care and simple human understanding.

With "The Lost Child" at least one clear pattern emerges in *Happiness*. In three different stories, the Catholic religion is the focal point for the emotional uncertainties and conflicts of Mary Lavin's characters. Father Hugh of "Happiness" makes a return appearance in "The Lost Child." His presence in the first and the last story in the collection has the effect of balancing the gallery of priests in *Happiness*. His gentleness and genuine concern for the feelings of others contrast sharply with the behavior of the miserly canon and the emotionally disturbed Father Patton. "A Pure Accident" and "The Lost Child" are similar, however, in their implied attitude toward the authority of the Church. In each story, the institution or the dogma of the Church seems harsh and unrealistic when it influences human emotions.

"A Pure Accident" and "The Lost Child" are also similar in narrative length. Both are examples of the novella form in Mary Lavin's fiction. The length of "A Pure Accident," however, seems more of a practical necessity than an aesthetic design because of the involved narrative events and the time lapse necessary to set up the story's conclusion. In "The Lost Child" the narrative is more compact and its effect is more intense than most of Mary Lavin's earlier attempts at the novella form. The action of the plot covers about three days, but most of the narrative focuses on a period of about twenty-four hours. This compression of time is a key factor in drawing attention to the emotional climate of the story rather than its plot. Thus "The Lost Child" fulfills Mary Lavin's own definition of the novella as opposed to the frustrated novel.

The impressionistic point of view is particularly effective in creating the intense atmosphere of "The Lost Child." In "Sunday Brings Sunday" and "What's Wrong with Aubretia?" the perspective carefully shifts from a third-person point of view, limited to the observation of the externalized thoughts and feelings of the main character, to a more impressionistic and intimate view of the character's inner state. The effect of this strategy is to create an emotional experience so intense that it momentarily breaks down the boundaries of external reality. The reader shares the stricken emotional states of Mona and Vera because the power of the experience is so strong that it transforms external reality into a symbol of their suffering.

In "The Lost Child" the impressionistic technique, rather than being saved for the story's emotional climax, is used on several occasions. The result is that external reality, as in stream-of-consciousness fiction, often gives way to the inner reality of the central character. Renée's thoughts and emotions are still described by a third-person narrator, but their flow usurps the mechanical movement of physical events at certain key moments. More the indirect interior monologue of Virginia Woolf than the direct interior monologue of Joyce's Penelope episode in *Ulysses*, the technique is used in scenes where there is little to distract Renée from her memories of the past. The first such moment comes immediately after Renée completes her conversion to the Roman Catholic faith. As she kneels in the pew, her thoughts are on the brevity of the ceremony and her children's disappointment in the routine nature of the occasion. Whatever her immediate concern and frustration, her awareness of the gravity of what she has done eventually provokes a series of memories closely associated with her conversion. She remembers the unhappiness of her family when she told them she was going to have a Catholic wedding. Though her mother finally accepted her decision, she still reacted bitterly to the news that her grandchildren would be baptized Catholics. The memory of her mother's hostility to her new faith stirs another memory of an equally bitter argument she had with Iris, her sister, on the subject of baptism. Though Iris always seemed comfortable with her Catholic friends, her antagonism toward Catholic dogma surfaced when she discovered that Cillin na Leanbh was a cemetery for unbaptized children. Only when Renée remembers that Father Hugh willingly arbitrated the debate over whether or not the Church still buried unbaptized children in unsanctified ground does she return to her immediate surroundings and her immediate worries:

And here she now was within the Church, having entrusted her full weight to it. But suddenly, with a start, she realized she had not said one prayer, had not offered one word of gratitude to God for the grace that had been bestowed on her. Yet she must have been on her knees for ages. The others were getting restless; the children were beginning to bicker wordlessly. (p. 112)

In this opening scene, Mary Lavin successfully executes what she believes is the first obligation of all good storytellers, to reveal all the background information the readers will need without boring them with a long exposition. Her usual strategy in her long fiction is similar to the one she uses in "The Lost Child." She learned that the best method was to allow the information to develop from within the dramatic situation of the opening narrative event. The difference in technique between "The Lost Child" and *The House in Clewe Street* is that the novella, unlike her first novel, develops its background material from within the mind of the main character. Thus the narrative flow of Renée's thoughts as she kneels in the pew is closer in concept to the impressionistic novels of Virginia Woolf than to Jane Austen's novels. The emotional association of past and present and the intimate observation of Renée's private thoughts and feelings make "The Lost Child" a modern story in form and content and one of Mary Lavin's most experimental in technique.

Shortly after Renée's reveries in the church, she has another opportunity to allow her mind to flow freely into the past. What
happens in between, however, not only influences the nature of the
memories, it also establishes the pattern of Renée's thoughts and
the dramatic action of the story. Once Renée, her family, and her
sister leave the church, their discussion of a place to eat lunch inadvertently leads to Renée's confession that she is pregnant once
again. Sensing her fatigue, her family decides to treat her to a ride
home by taxi while they stay in the city for lunch. Once in the cab,
Renée's thoughts naturally flow back to her earlier pregnancies.
Unlike her memories of her difficulties with her mother and Iris
over Catholic dogma, her thoughts about her pregnancies are happy
ones. She remembers how her husband Mike pampered her, how
proud he was of the way she prepared herself for childbirth. After
her pleasing memories of the health of her babies, she speculates
happily on the sex of the expected child. Rejecting the thought of
scientific efforts to predict the sex of the child, she lapses into a
blissful peace in which the flow of her feelings blends naturally with
the bloodstream connecting the child and herself.

Therefore by the time Renée is brought back to more immediate
concerns by the cab jolting to a stop, the narrative has established
an associative pattern out of her physical movement and her
memories of the past. Her conversion, her pregnancy, and the
sharply contrasting memories of her sister's bitter reaction to Cillin
na Leanbh and her husband's tender response to her first pregnancy
weave an emotional and symbolic fabric around the expected child.
What follows in "The Lost Child" is tragic in itself, but Renée's
miscarriage takes on a terrible inevitability when seen within the intricate narrative design.

After Renée returns to the farm, she learns that during her
absence one of the local farmers dumped a load of manure at the
end of her garden. Fearing that the manure will smother some of
her plants, she works frantically to move the pile away from the garden. Unfortunately, because of her pregnancy, she becomes so
nauseated by the powerful smell and the sight of the worms oozing
about in the dung that she becomes hysterical. Though calmed immediately by the returning Mike and Iris, Renée still worries that
she has overextended herself. Her struggle with the manure pile, in
itself a provocative symbol of the richness and corruption of life,
foreshadows the approaching crisis that she has instigated. Her concern about the child takes on a new and ominous reality when she

discovers a few hours later that she is spotting. By the next day, she begins to hemorrhage.

Though Renée's struggle with the manure pile and her resultant miscarriage are narrated in a brutally realistic manner, the narrative still retains its intricate pattern by returning to an impressionistic viewpoint at key moments in the story. As Renée is taken to the hospital in an ambulance, she experiences the strange and vivid sensation that the soft pulp passing out of her body is actually all her vital parts, and that she has made the remarkable discovery that she can go on living after being emptied of liver, kidneys, lungs, and heart. In the hospital she has an equally strange dream in which she encounters two men digging a hole. Not surprisingly, the men are about to bury a baby lying by the hole. Once she understands what the men are going to do, she tries to cry out against them. Though she cannot utter a sound to stop the burial, she does undergo a dream experience similar to her earlier sensation of floating away:

"I tried to cry out and stop them but no sound came—you know how that happens in a dream but they weren't able to lift the baby. They kept trying and trying but they couldn't and then I realized the baby wasn't made of flesh and blood at all, because I would see through it. It was like a soap bubble—only it was alive. I saw the grass through it, and the crocuses. I know it sounds silly, but I was happy because I knew then they couldn't put it in the clay. I thought it might even float away into the sky—" (pp. 147 - 48)

Renée's emotional ordeal and her haunting dreams form another associative pattern in "The Lost Child." Together, they reveal the perpetual struggle between physical reality and spiritual aspiration. Renée's desperate effort to prevent the dung from smothering her garden and her futile attempt to stop her miscarriage are strong indications that physical events easily play havoc with the human need for love and order. Renée's dreams, however, are equally strong statements of the human spirit's refusal to accept its mortality even in the face of tragedy. When Renée tells her husband that she is worried about the immortal soul of the lost child, she draws together the major patterns in the story because her fretfulness also reflects her earlier memories of the resistance of her mother and sister to Catholic ritual and dogma. The narrative effect of returning to the emotional implications of the earlier pattern is to draw attention to the problems for the human spirit if it accepts a narrow and rigid notion of an afterlife. Even as it reaches out for some definitive haven, the soul is capable of creating nightmarish spiritual technicalities, thereby denying itself a state of bliss.

The conflicts between physical and spiritual realities and the questions about the health and destiny of the human soul are resolved in the final scene of "The Lost Child." When Mike sees how upset Renée is about the miscarriage, he brings Father Hugh to the hospital. At first, the priest tries to comfort her with theology. His statement, however, that there is a growing body of opinion in the Church opposing the theory of Limbo does not satisfy her. Nor does she respond favorably to his suggestion that the doctor might have performed a medical baptism—Iris is shocked at the idea. Only when Father Hugh offers to sit down with Mike, Iris, and Renée and thrash things out does Renée respond again to the life around her. She becomes sensitive to the emotional atmosphere of the room, to Mike and Iris's deep concern about her health, to Father Hugh's concern for her spirit, and to her own need to love Mike no matter what religious technicalities interfere with their lives. As in "Happiness," the theme of human love and understanding emerges to counter whatever physical suffering does to diminish the desire to continue the business of living. As Renée relaxes within the comforting circle of good feeling that surrounds her, the room, in her mind's eye, becomes transfixed by light. This halo of love and sympathy, similar to the one that surrounds Mrs. Ramsey's dinner party in *To the Lighthouse*, ends "The Lost Child" on a note of mature optimism that overcomes the tragic sorrow of the lost child.

IV   A Memory and Other Stories.

A Memory continues the autobiographical pattern of Mary Lavin's later fiction. In "Trastevere" and "Villa Violetta," Mary Lavin returns to the character of Vera Traske. Both stories are based upon her experiences in Florence during the period of her first Guggenheim. The more personal of the two stories, "Villa Violetta" also repeats the theme of mature optimism which appears so forcefully in "Happiness" and "The Lost Child." In "Tomb of an Ancestor," the opening story in the collection, the autobiographical material is less contemporary. The setting for this story of childhood adventure and discovery is drawn from her memories of Athenry, the Castlerampart of her earlier fiction: "The town was once encircled by a rampart. This in part was fallen, but deep in the town's core was an inner wall, intact except for one gap. Inside this again was the ruin of an old friary and an ancient burial ground long closed to funerals."[6]

The Mahons' mercantile life in Athenry is also a significant part of the background of "Tomb of an Ancestor." The children that play together are from rival shopkeeping families, the Duffys and the Dermodys. As a matter of fact, the Dermodys, the more prosperous family, bear the name of the American relatives visited by Nora just before her meeting with Tom Lavin on the boat returning to Ireland. Mickser, one of the Dermody children, has the same name as the antagonistic youth in "The Living." As in the earlier story, Mickser agitates others into some adventure outside their familiar territory.

Other than its value as a nostalgic return to the fictional world of Castlerampart, "Tomb of an Ancestor" plays no major role in Mary Lavin's fiction. The story resembles "The Living" and "One Evening" in its attempt to extend its theme beyond the innocent world of childhood. The encounter with the adult world, however, is more in keeping with the general theme suggested in the title of the collection and in the nostalgic nature of the story's setting and background. "The Tomb of an Ancestor," as the title suggests, is a journey into an emotional past, evoked by the ghostly memories of the tragic love affair between Vinny Dermody and Ada Duffy. Cleverly conceived, the story, however, lacks the deep emotional experience of her finest stories because it relies on the formula of the story with a pattern. Most of the plot has to do with a mad race between the Dermody and Duffy forces to find the graves of their ancestors in the old cemetery. The plot takes its unusual twist when the Dermodys discover that the marble tomb containing the names of Vinny and other ancestors bears the name Duffy. At first baffled by the discovery, Molly, Mickser's cousin, understands the reason for their mistake, that their great-grandmother, who married one of her own shopboys, must have been a Duffy. The full ramifications of all this are that Vinny and Ada could not marry because they were cousins, that all the Duffys and Dermodys are distant relatives, and that Mickser and Milly, who are very close to each other, could repeat the tragedy of Vinny and Ada in the near future. The ending is clever, impressive, and contrived.

"Trastevere" and "Villa Violetta" are Mary Lavin's Italian stories. The appearance of Vera Traske in both stories clearly underlines their autobiographical nature. In "Trastevere," Mrs.

Traske is a middle-aged novelist who has just returned from a trip to
Italy. On her first day in New York, she comes across Paul Martin, a
young man she met during her stay in Rome. The surprise of seeing
Paul turns into shock when she hears about the suicide of Della
Carr. The coincidental encounter and the news of Della's death
form the setting for the story within a story of Mrs. Traske's only
meeting with this intense and demanding woman. After she leaves
her young friend, she remembers the evening in Rome when Paul
escorted her to the Carr's apartment in Trastevere. Hoping to find
some key to explain Della's suicide, she carefully examines the deep
impression the evening and her hostess made upon her.

What emerges from Mrs. Traske's memory of Trastevere is the
portrait of a hauntingly beautiful young woman admired for her independent nature. Mrs. Traske remembers, however, that her initial
impression of Della as a "Maypole, festooned with ribbons, which,
as they gyrated, bound the young men closer and closer to her" (p.
50) was entirely wrong. After observing her erratic behavior at
dinner, she realized the absurdity of her Maypole image. Rather
than tolerating Paul's and her husband, Simon's, dependency, Della
appeared to thrive upon it. Any gesture of independence on the part
of someone else was met quickly by an intimidating stare or in-
sidious remark. Remembering Simon's refusal to eat his *osso bucco*
after his wife sampled it and Della's demand that he eat it for lunch
the next day, Mrs. Traske finally gains a fleeting insight into the
tension between the Carrs and the nature of Della's troubled
emotions.

The story of Della is interesting as a Jamesian study of the secret
passions which manipulate even the most sophisticated and intelligent lives. The final outcome of "Trastevere," however, has a
significant autobiographical side to it. The tragic fate of the Carrs
forces Mrs. Traske, once again portrayed as a widow, into a reap-
praisal of a deeply satisfying relationship she has found late in her
life. Now able to recognize more clearly the value of what she and
Mack have to give each other, she reconsiders her decision to avoid
marriage again. Autobiographically, Mrs. Traske's intimate
relationship with Mack and her hesitancy to commit herself again to
marriage reflect Mary Lavin's situation with Michael Scott. Her
own deeply satisfying relationship, which developed in the years
after William Walsh's death, went through the same critical phase
described in "Trastevere." Like her fictional counterpart, Mary
Lavin decided that with so much to give each other she would
marry Michael Scott after he received laicization from the Church.

"Villa Violetta" is a much more openly autobiographical story than "Trastevere." Much of the first part of the plot is drawn directly from Mary Lavin's personal experiences in Florence while she was on her first Guggenheim. The unfortunate results of her decision to travel abroad with her daughters are reflected in Vera Traske's confusion and frustration during her early days in Florence. With three young children in hand and no husband to help her, she quickly discovers the vulnerability of her position: "She had no warning that Florence would appear in no better light than any other city in which a young widow arrived alone with three small children, very little of the language, and no grasp at all of the currency" (p. 97).

Another indication of the autobiographical nature of "Villa Violetta" is its similarity to "Happiness" in characterization and theme. Though the dead husband's name has been changed from Robert to Richard (the name used in "In a Café" and "In the Middle of the Fields"), the children's names remain the same, and Vera's professional life as a writer is clearly established. Once again the youngest child is named Linda; the second-oldest, Bea; and the oldest daughter (the unnamed narrator of "Happiness"), Gloria. In "Trastevere," Gloria is also the name of the daughter who accompanies Mrs. Traske on her dinner visit to Della and Simon Carr. Vera's difficulty in adapting to the Italian language, currency, and climate is closely related to her failure to find any time for her writing. Between her unsuccessful efforts to find a suitable apartment for her needs and a school for her girls, she has not been able to write a single line. At one point, she confesses that her special problem, other than being a widow with three young children, is her doubt about her writing. Her reason for coming to Florence is to restore the confidence in her work she has lacked since Richard's death. Unfortunately, her situation in Italy is even worse than it was in Ireland.

Another autobiographical feature of "Villa Violetta" is the priest-tourist guide, Father Tom. As his name suggests, he is a combination of Tom Lavin and Michael Scott. His role in "Villa Violetta" is the same as Father Hugh's in "Happiness" and "The Lost Child." Warm and compassionate, he gives Vera the help and understanding she needs to return to her writing. Acting upon Vera in the same fashion as Michael Scott acted upon Mary Lavin in her difficult years after William Walsh's death, Father Tom not only gives her the emotional reassurance she needs to resume her career, he satisfies her practical needs by finding a way to eliminate her financial burdens. A story with a strong autobiographical pattern, "Villa Violetta" repeats the basic message of "Happiness." The real value of Father Tom's concern and generosity is the atmosphere it creates to help Vera open herself to life again. Once she renews what Nick Carraway would have called her readiness for life, Vera has only to turn to the one task that has given her the greatest sense of fulfillment in her life.

Mary Lavin once observed that some of her longer stories are flawed because they really are two stories in one.[7] "Villa Violetta" is a prime example of this kind of story. While Vera's personal problems are being solved by Father Tom, her youngest daughter helps Father Tom solve his own problem. During his party's earlier visit to St. Peter's, a young girl suffered a serious attack of vertigo. Since then she has remained in a coma in spite of Father Tom's efforts to reach her. What Linda does is to draw Peggy back into life through her own innocent desire for companionship. She gives the young girl exactly what Father Tom gives her mother. Her unselfish act also fulfills Father Tom's prophecy that one good act begets others. It has the final effect of rounding off the narrative of "Villa Violetta." Unfortunately, rather than enhancing the narrative, it does little more than impose a truth upon the ending, turning "Villa Violetta" into a story with a pattern. Interesting from an autobiographical standpoint, the story falls short of the artistry of her best fiction.

"Asigh" and "A Memory" break the autobiographical pattern of *A Memory*. They are also the best-written stories in the collection. What they share with "Tomb of an Ancestor," "Trastevere," and "Villa Violetta" is the theme of the burden of the past upon human lives. As a study of the oppressive emotional ties between father and daughter, "Asigh" also resembles "What's Wrong with Aubretia?" and "One Summer." Told from the third-person limited perspective of the daughter, the story begins just before the father's death. The opening scene quickly establishes the emotional tension between father and daughter. She feels afraid of him even as he lies helplessly on his deathbed. On the other hand, the father's feelings are a mixture of concerned guilt and angry rationalization of his past treatment of his daughter. The single event responsible for this atmosphere of fear and guilt is associated with an ugly, festering sore on the daughter's leg. Once alone, she remembers how her father discovered her talking with one of the hired men, and how he raised the head-collar and struck her twice, as if she were one of his beasts.

Once the terrible memory of the blows passes from her mind, the narrative traces the events leading up to the beating. Strangely, her remembrances of her early life with her father are pleasant ones. Whatever her present feelings, she recalls the closeness between them and her father's great pride in her attractive appearance and her vivacious nature. The flaw in their relationship, however, was also contained in his admiration of her attractiveness and his belief that his daughter inherited his own passionate nature, that "sparkle" in his eye. Suspicious and possessive, he watches her closely when she talks to the hired help, for fear that he will lose the daughter he hopes to auction off some day to the highest bidder.

The arrival of Tod Mallon, the new owner of the farm next to them, sets in motion the sequence of events leading up to the beating. He works out an unspoken agreement with her father to marry her sometime in the future. Rather than resenting the arrangement, she looks forward to the time when her feelings "could be shared with another soul" (p. 75). Ironically, when the terrible scene with her father takes place, she is talking to the hired man about her future life with Tod Mallon. Mistakenly assuming that she is flirting, her father lashes out at her with the head-collar. Disappointed that she is not with Mallon and shamed by her plea not to beat her in public, he strikes the second damaging blow more out of his own frustration and resentment of being wrong than out of his sense of paternal justice.

What follows in "Asigh" is a summary of the sad and bitter years following the beating. Her ulcerated leg prevents her from marrying Mallon because she cannot perform the heavy duties demanded of a farmer's wife. The only satisfaction she has is knowing that Mallon refuses to take another wife. When her father finally dies, she hears Mallon's own bitter confession that her father's blows hurt him emotionally as much as it damaged her physically. So many years have passed, however, that the words spoken admit a truth that has passed them by: "At last—at last—after all these years it was said. Not in the words of youth. Not in the way she would once have wanted to hear it—but in the only way it could be said now. She looked at him in pity" (p. 90).

After her father's death, her only hope for fulfillment lies in encouraging the relationship between Flossie and her younger brother, Tom. Her desire to have nieces and nephews gathered around her to compensate for the lost opportunity for sons and daughters is crushed, however, by Tom's revelation that he and Flossie have been secretly married for years. The discovery that

their marriage has been barren is the final blow. All through Mary
Lavin's fiction the relentless and oppressive nature of time has
tormented her characters, denying them hope and peace of mind.
There is no more effective revelation of the devastating influence of
time in her fiction, however, than that which appears in the final
image of "Asigh." The terrible knowledge of the story's protagonist,
that she is condemned to a lonely death in spite of her past dreams
and hopes for the future, finds its objective correlative in the time-
laden image of Tom doing the one thing in his empty life that gives
him some pleasure:

> She looked down towards the river-field. It was almost too dark to see Tom,
> and it must have been too dark for him to see what he was doing, but he
> was still swinging the scythe expertly from side to side, slicing through the
> reeds and the wild grasses, with a gesture so true and natural it might have
> been a branch swaying in the wind. (pp. 95 - 96)

Thematically and technically, "A Memory" is an important story
in Mary Lavin's career. It treats the emotional differences which
separate human beings no matter how they try to protect
themselves against their own natures. James and Myra believe they
have the perfect situation. A research professor, James takes pride in
the intellectual character of their relationship. Not actually married,
he still feels that with Myra he has entered into a marriage of
minds. The verbal exactitude of their conversations, the truthfulness
of their sentiments, the special connotation they give to the word
love, all point to a blissful human relationship free of the usual
emotional complications.

Mary Lavin's narrative strategy in "A Memory" is to open the
story from a third-person point of view, limited to James's perception of his relationship with Myra. The concept of a limited point of
view is supported by James's narrow understanding of the full
nature of his arrangement with Myra. Like a Lambert Strether,
James sees the world only from within the narrow range of his own
moral and intellectual interests. Unfortunately for James, no matter
how he tries to avoid emotional situations, he still has to contend
with them even within the sanctified domain of his cottage
hideaway. On this particular day, his will to work on the manuscript
of his *magnum opus* on the creative process is undermined by his
own nervous exhaustion and the reluctance of his mind to focus on
anything except physical matters. He decides that a visit to Myra in

Dublin is just the sort of intellectual tonic that he needs before he resumes his work.

In his unsettled state of mind, James not only turns to his clean and blissful relationship with Myra, he also remembers his brief, emotionally disturbing affair with one of his students. His memory of the violence of his feelings for Emmy contrasts sharply with his conception of his intellectual love for Myra. Curiously, his thoughts about Emmy also establish a narrative link between "Asigh" and "A Memory." The previous summer James had learned that some people named Balfe had purchased Asigh House. At first not making the connection between the name and Emmy, he finally remembers her marriage to a Balfe when he sees her drive by in a car. His discovery that his former sweetheart, now married and the mother of several children, is his neighbor will take on great importance later in the narrative. The initial significance, however, is to draw the emotional events of "Asigh" into the narrative of "A Memory," if only by implication. In "Asigh" Tom's suggestion to his sister that they would be better off selling Asigh House becomes a reality in "A Memory." None of the characters from "Asigh" appears or is even mentioned in "A Memory," but the emotional link between the characters of the two stories is a strong one. In both cases, seemingly perfect arrangements (one potential, the other actual) are destroyed by a violent show of emotion. In spite of James's self-assurance about his relationship with Myra, he undergoes a physical and emotional ordeal that in its own way is as severe as the pain and shame imposed upoon the unfortunate protagonist of "Asigh."

James's ordeal actually begins when he decides to forsake his work for a trip to Dublin and a comforting visit with Myra. Reluctant to come to her apartment before his usual time, he spends a dreary and aimless day wandering about the city. His decision to avoid catching Myra by surprise, however, proves his undoing. When Myra finds out that James has been in Dublin all day without calling her, she reacts in a manner completely at odds with James's image of her. When his partner in a marriage of minds begins to talk about his insensitivity to her needs and all the sacrifices that she has made over the years, James is shocked by this uncharacteristic outburst of self-pity. At the end of a day of nervous exhaustion and disturbing influences from his past life, James's well-ordered, intellectual existence is washed away by a torrent of female emotion.

At this critical point in the narrative, Mary Lavin's strategy is to

shift the perspective to Myra's point of view. Whatever James
thought about Myra's nature it is clear from her thoughts that she
feels she has been forced to "denature" herself to fit his limited
needs. His failure to tell her that he was in Dublin earlier in the day
is simply the catalyst, releasing her intense feeling that she will
never be able to change him or to express her emotions to him
without fearing his repulsion: "Tonight it seemed that his
emotional capacity was completely dried up. Despair overcame her.
She'd never change him now. He was fixed in his faults, cemented
into his barren way of life" (p. 196). In a rare moment in Mary
Lavin's stories, a female character speaks out against the injustices
of a male world in which the female is forced to cater to the male
even if it means denying her own nature. When she tells James that
he has denatured her, she feels her words prompted by forces even
stronger than her own aroused feelings. Indeed, she speaks for all
the women who have suffered from the insensitivity and treachery
of males, and perhaps for woman writers who have endured
obscurity because their stories have not appealed to males:

It was as if, out of the corners of the room she was being prompted by the
voices of all the women in the world who'd ever been let down, or fancied
themselves badly treated. The room vibrated with their whispers. Go on,
they prompted. Tell him what you think of him. Don't let him get away
with it. He has got off long enough. To stop the voices she stuck her fingers
into her ears, but the voices only got louder. She had to shout them down.
(p. 197)

James's reaction to the tears, accusations, and hysteria, once he
recovers from the initial shock, is to flee the apartment. Once the
scene shifts from the apartment to the street, the narrative view
returns to James's wounded perspective. Though he tries to recover
his mental balance, James keeps thinking about their common row.
Complicating his situation is the fact that he has not eaten since
morning. When he tries to find a quiet place, he learns that he has
lost touch with Dublin. Frustrated once again in his quest for peace
and relaxation, his only remaining desire is to return to his cottage.
Once aboard the bus, however, he gets into a disagreement with the
conductor and ends up on a dark road at least two miles from his
cottage.
    What follows in "A Memory" is a devastating conclusion to an
already disastrous day for James. His disturbed mental state is

already matched by nausea and chest pains. While wandering through the woods looking for the path to his cottage, his emotional and physical aggravation reaches a dangerous point. The final scene in "A Memory" has an ironic relationship with one of the most famous scenes in Fitzgerald's *The Great Gatsby*. Like Jay Gatsby, James follows a faint green light which he feels will safely bring him the bliss he has unsuccessfully sought all day. As in *The Great Gatsby*, the green light comes to symbolize the unattainable goal of recapturing the past. Because James finds himself in the Asigh wood, he associates the light with the Balfes. After losing his bearings several times and falling heavily to the ground, he becomes delirious. Exhausted by his futile efforts to find his way out of the woods, he finally collapses in terrible pain and confusion. In his state of delirium, the green light becomes the "light of life itself" (p. 222). Finally, fearing that he is dying, James gives the light the name of the one person in his life who penetrated his stuffiness and pride. He calls out to Emmy to save him from his terrible fate. Unfortunately, like Gatsby, James cannot bring back the past or rely upon past feelings to give him the strength to survive his ordeal. In one last effort, he tries to focus his efforts on finding Myra. The present, however, is as barren of help as the past. Emotionally and intellectually defeated, James, with his last dying breath, accomplishes nothing more than sucking rotted leaves into his mouth.

What Mary Lavin accomplishes in "A Memory" is one of the most sophisticated treatments of the major theme of her fiction. Most of her stories are studies of the terrible loneliness of people even within the closest possible relationships. Alienated either because of a difference in temperament or a flaw in character, husband and wife, father and daughter, brother and sister, all experience the same disappointments and the same bitter feelings of emptiness and failure. If a couple, in spite of their differences, gain a moment of bliss, they also run the risk of having their happiness ripped from them by some cruel stroke of nature. In her widow stories, however, Mary Lavin also observes the capacity in some individuals to endure their personal ordeals and to struggle forward with their lives. Her Vera character embodies this particular attitude and strength. What emerges as a final vision, then, is a recognition that life with all its snares and emotional pitfalls still represents the only chance that people have for love and understanding. Mary Lavin's strongest characters commit themselves to love, endure their personal tragedies, and never give up the struggle for life until assured that life is finished with them. Her weakest characters, like James, find that life is too much for them. All they can do is curse their life and wait for death.

CHAPTER 6

The Influences:
A World View of Literature

I Mary Lavin and Irish Literature

MARY Lavin's contemporaries have had little trouble recognizing what Benedict Kiely has called her "undoubted
genius."[1] There has been general agreement, a rare event among
writers, that she has a remarkable talent for describing the world of
ordinary experience. She has also been praised for her understanding of the complexities of the human heart. In the preface to her
first collection of short stories, Lord Dunsany states his unequivocal
admiration for her realism, the way in which she portrays the quite
ordinary lives "of people who many might suppose have no story in
all their experiences."[2] Frank O'Connor, often praised as a master
of the Irish short story, finds in Mary Lavin's stories "an authentici-
ty and solidity that make the work of most Irish writers seem
shadowy."[3] In his introduction to *Collected Stories*, V. S. Pritchett
summarizes most of the earlier views of Mary Lavin's stories by
singling out her sympathy and truthfulness, her insight into the
human heart, and her controlled revelation of strong emotions: "I
cannot think of any Irish writer who has gone so profoundly without
fear into the Irish heart. This fearlessness makes her remarkable."[4]

Literary critics have expressed the same admiration for Mary
Lavin's fiction. In his pioneer study, "A Skeleton Key to the Stories
of Mary Lavin," Augustine Martin stresses her tireless investigation
of the Irish middle class, which gives her "a unique position in the
Irish short story."[5] Noting her critical neglect, he feels that she has
suffered from an "extra-literary concern" which is more a part of
"the history of publicity than the history of literature."[6] Robert W.
Caswell has been the most active Lavin critic. Not only has Caswell
argued convincingly that Mary Lavin's understanding of "the

143

human heart's vagaries"is unequaled in contemporary Irish fiction, he has drawn a close and favorable comparison between the characters in her work and those in Joyce's *Dubliners*. Like Augustine Martin, Robert Caswell has also recognized that Mary Lavin has been "relegated to a critical limbo" for extraliterary reasons. Caswell believes that her work has been neglected because it is not a reflection of Irish politics and nationalism. In spite of presumed critical views about the character of Irish literature, a volume like *Tales from Bective Bridge* is "as important in its way as those which O'Connor singles out in *The Lonely Voice:* Moore's *The Untilled Field,* Joyce's *Dubliners,* and O'Flaherty's *Spring Sowing*—as important, but of course not as influential."[7]

Though Mary Lavin's work has been badly neglected in Ireland and America, the first dissertation solely devoted to her fiction appeared in 1968 and the first book-length study in 1975. Both critical studies stress the universal nature and appeal of her themes. Bobbie Jean Roark, in her dissertation, "Mary Lavin: The Local and the Universal," traces the development of her large themes, death and bereavement, love and marriage, within a tightly controlled local setting. Zack Bowen in his book for the Irish Writers Series establishes her "all pervasive theme" of "freedom, or lack of it," which is apparent in "Mary Lavin's lifelong concern with practicalities, money problems, responsibilities, and the effects of death" and her "acute awareness of social class, and society's sanctions and rules."[8] Bowen, too, is very much aware of the critical neglect of Mary Lavin's fiction: "That her work has not received the critical attention it deserves is due in some measure to the precision and clarity of her style and vision, which embarrass criticism and offer little to occupy the attention of contemporary textual explicators."[9]

Bowen's view to the contrary, most critics believe that Mary Lavin's work has been neglected because it does not fit into preconceived notions of Irish literature. Though she is often compared to O'Flaherty, O'Connor, and O'Faolain by reviewers, her stories simply do not deal with the same subject matter or express the same interest in Irish political life. As a matter of fact, she is not even a part of the same literary generation as O'Flaherty, O'Connor, and O'Faolain. O'Flaherty was born in 1897, O'Faolain in 1900, and O'Connor in 1903. All three writers were young men during the time of revolution and civil war in Ireland, and their stories obviously reflect the profound influence of the violent and tragic

events leading up to Ireland's independence and the inevitable dis-
illusionment of the postrevolutionary period. Mary Lavin was born
in 1912 in America. She did not even see Ireland until 1921, when
she left America with her mother to settle in the small town of
Athenry with her mother's people. Once she overcame her longing
for America, Mary Lavin turned her attention not to Ireland's
political troubles but to the members of her family and the people
of Athenry. "The Patriot Son," Mary Lavin's one story about
revolutionary Ireland, so disturbed Frank O'Connor because of its
criticism of both sides of the conflict that he wrote, as mentioned
previously, that "from a patriotic point of view" one Lavin story
about political revolution "is more than enough."[10] As far as her
other stories are concerned, the Irish reader "might as well be
reading Turgenev or Leskov for the first time, overwhelmed by the
material unfamiliarity of the whole background, versts, shubas,
roubles, and patronymics."[11]

O'Connor's emphasis on the foreign nature of Mary Lavin's
stories and his specific reference to Russian materials is close to
Lord Dunsany's early comparison of Mary Lavin's stories to the un-
compromising realism of Russian fiction. O'Connor sees Mary
Lavin's fiction as foreign, however, because it does not reflect the
Ireland he writes about in his stories. This view is as wrongheaded
as his statement that a woman's basic role during a time of political
revolution is either to stay at home or to bring food to the prison
gate. According to O'Connor, an Irish writer has no business writing
about anything other than that which is dictated by the political
climate of the country. As for women, they seem to have no
business writing at all, what with bread to bake and children to care
for.

O'Connor's comments in "The Girl at the Gaol Gate" give some
idea of the difficulties Mary Lavin has faced throughout her literary
career. Not only has she been victimized by a traditional prejudice
against woman writers that has forced some to use male names
while reducing others to critical obscurity, she has also been unfairly judged on the basis of a view of Irish literature as the sole property of rebels and exiles. There is no question of the powerful influence of the figures and events from Ireland's political history
upon modern Irish literature. Yet to deny Mary Lavin a place in
modern Irish literature simply because her stories do not fit a
preconceived literary pattern is to impose the same form of cen-
sorship upon her work that modern Irish writers have bitterly en-

dured both before and since the end of British rule. This is not to say that her work is entirely outside the mainstream of Irish life. Besides the stories that make deliberate use of Irish dialect, setting, and character types, her fiction usually portrays the Irish middle class. To say that her stories are not Irish is to say that there is no middle class in Ireland.

Once granting Mary Lavin her world of shopkeepers, clerks, farmers, domestic types, and lonely widows, critics have discovered the intricate craft of her fiction. Thomas J. Murray, for example, describes Mary Lavin's characters as "the small crabbed people one associates with small dingy shops."[12] The reader grudgingly accepts them "in their ordinariness as he might accept some annoying and unnameable irritation."[13] After pointing out this reader's bias, however, Murray goes on to describe the "admirable control" of her point of view which frees her stories from "stuck-on social issues as background scenery of cliché ideas of 'Irishness' as ingredients of characterization."[14] While rejecting preconceived notions of Irish subject matter, Augustine Martin has discovered the five Grimes stories which appeared in three separate volumes over a period of about twelve years. Martin's view, that these stories are "typical of her milieu . . . of Irish middle-class existence,"[15] is highly significant because they are also a part of a larger pattern of stories which create an imaginary world out of Mary Lavin's early life in Athenry. Castlerampart, her fictional name for Athenry, appears like an Irish Yoknapatawpha in her stories. It is the landscape for *The House in Clewe Street*, the Grimes stories, and many of her finest short stories and novellas. Within this commonplace setting for her ordinary characters, Mary Lavin penetrates the surface of mediocrity, and exposes the dark and terrible currents of loneliness which haunt her characters.

Besides Mary Lavin's imaginary world of Castlerampart, there are several key patterns woven out of her characters and dramatic situations. The Grimes stories are united by character and narrative, but many other stories have similar ties. The Vera stories offer rich and complex variations on the themes of alienation and widowhood. Other stories are linked by the repeated appearance of a single character. Naida Paston, Father Hugh, Jasper Kane, Eamon Og, and Mickser are among a gallery of characters who play key roles in more than one story. Naida Paston, for example, is the central character in the childhood drama of "Limbo," while in "The Convert" her death is the cause of the emotional outburst which suddenly exposes the empty life of her former suitor. There are also stories linked by dramatic situations, some actually appearing as continuations or variations of earlier stories. "Bridal Sheets" is both an alteration and extension of "The Green Grave and the Black Grave." "One Summer" continues the emotional drama of "What's Wrong with Aubretia?" to its bitter conclusion, while "A Memory" has an intriguing geographical and thematic link with "Asigh." Rather than a loose collection of stories covering several decades of her career, Mary Lavin's fiction is a rich mosaic of literary patterns woven out of landscape, character, and theme.

II *Mary Lavin and World Literature*

Though Mary Lavin's subject matter is as Irish as the town of Athenry, the form of her fiction is indebted to sources more Russian, English, and American than Irish. Benedict Kiely has identified one particularly Irish characteristic of her stories, her tendency to introduce an element of fantasy into her otherwise realistic studies of the middle class. This characteristic, however, lies on the periphery of her fiction. As effective as the technique can be in stories like "The Becker Wives," with its spritelike Flora, and "The Cuckoo-spit," with its echoes of the Dierdre myth, Mary Lavin's fiction is basically made up of what Kiely calls "her quiet terrifyingly intimate studies of domesticity."[16]

Mary Lavin's early admirers compared her to the Russian writers. Later critics have noted the resemblance between her work and the short stories of that European Irishman James Joyce as well as Katherine Mansfield, Henry James (the European American), and Flannery O'Connor. As noted earlier, when asked if she saw herself as "part of a tradition of Irish writers," Mary Lavin gave the obvious answer that because she was an Irishwoman her "raw material was Irish."[17] She went on, however, to lend her own support to the view that her work extends beyond the stream of Irish literature:

Anything I wanted to achieve was in the traditions of world literature. I did not read the Irish writers until I had already dedicated myself to the short story. Then I would have been a fool not to have studied them, masters as they were of the medium. I studied English and French in college and outside the curriculum I read widely among the Russians and the Americans. O'Connor, O'Faolain, and O'Flaherty were only a part of literature as I thought of it. I had read Tchekov and Tourgeniev, Flaubert and Joyce and the shorter works of D. H. Lawrence, Tolstoy, and Henry James. As for influences perhaps I owed most to Edith Wharton, the pastoral works of George Sand, and especially Sarah Orne Jewett.[18]

Mary Lavin's comment reinforces the critical view that her conception of the short story owes far more to "the traditions of world literature" than to the nationalism of Irish literature. In the preface to *Selected Stories*, she offers some views on literature that further support the broader critical treatment of her fiction. She begins the preface with a brief episode from her childhood, recalling a visit with her father to an old Dublin watchmaker to have a small gold watch repaired. Seeing the old man's hands trembling with an ague, she feared for the safety of her watch until her father guided the watchmaker's hands to his task: "Oh but the fixity, the sureness of those fingers when once they entered the intricate world of their craft."[19]

After playfully offering her childhood memory as an apology for devoting her life to the art of fiction, she develops the story of the watchmaker into a parable of the writer and "the mystery of imaginative creation."[20] His trembling hands become the symbol of the writer's insecurity outside the world of the imagination, while his sureness of craft represents the writer's imaginative vision and dedication. The episode also gives Mary Lavin the opportunity to discuss the critical relationship between the imagination and memory and the important advantage that the short-story writer enjoys over the novelist. First of all, she states her belief in the supremacy of the intuitive imagination. Whatever the artistic purpose, the imagination is the source of the controlling vision, the way in which the writer perceives the world of feeling, where "the vagaries and contrarieties there to be found have their own integral design."[21] By claiming that she lives too intensely in the moment to work deliberately at constructing a fictional world out of stored observations and memories, Mary Lavin stresses a philosophy of art similar to Virginia Woolf's. She also recognizes, however, that memory, often a burden to the writer, also plays an important role in the creative process. While giving up the raw materials and practical design for the work of art, it also imposes a discipline and selectivity upon it. The form of the work develops out of the writer's intuitive perception of the vague and contrary world of human feeling, but the content of the work is largely dependent upon experiences and memories.

Having developed her thoughts on the relationship of imagination and memory into a Jamesian needle-and-thread view of the inseparability of form and content, Mary Lavin concludes her essay with a discussion of the advantage of the short story over the novel. She points out that she turned to the short story out of necessity rather than choice because of the demands of her family life. Confessing her early resentment of domestic responsibilities and her family's indifference to her work, she states her firm belief that her difficulties imposed a discipline that acted favorably upon her "often feverish, overfertile imagination."[22] What she learned was the superiority of the short story over the novel as the art form in which "a writer distills the essence of his thought."[23]

Rather than satisfying artificial requirements of brevity and relevance, the true short story is a happy balance of form and content, achieved when the intuitive imagination works in harmony with the materials involuntarily received from the memory and the artifices deliberately selected by the writer to make the story striking or appealing. All that remains to make the imaginative experience complete is for the story to enter the region of the mind and heart, for the reader to experience the same profound sense of truth that inspired the writing of the story. Mary Lavin ends her theory of the creative imagination with her own variations on the Yeatsian paradox of the creative process: "To whom does the story belong; to the writer or to the reader for whom it was written? To whom does the echo belong; to the horn or to the valley?"[24]

Mary Lavin's statements in the preface suggest the influence of two writers on her work that she failed to mention in her *St. Stephen's* interview. Though Henry James seems to be the guiding force behind her ideas on the marriage of form and content, Virginia Woolf and Katherine Mansfield are the keys to Mary Lavin's views on the value of intuition and feeling in the literary process and the importance of truth as the writer's aim. It is not surprising that Virginia Woolf's art would influence Mary Lavin's conception of writing. She wrote her first story while in the process of completing her doctoral thesis on Virginia Woolf. Though her work is rarely as experimental, it reflects the same view of fiction as an imaginative re-creation of the complexities of life rather than an arranged criticism of life. Mary Lavin's carefully drawn studies of ordinary people whose loneliness and despair briefly flare up within their commonplace lives offer graphic support for Virginia Woolf's well-known statement on the relationship between art and life:

Examine for a moment an ordinary mind on an ordinary day. The mind
receives a myriad of impressions—trivial, fantastic, evanescent, or engraved
with the sharpness of steel. From all sides they come, an incessant shower
of innumerable atoms; and as they fall, as they shape themselves into the
life of Monday or Tuesday, the accent falls differently from of old; the moment of importance came not here but there; so that if a writer were a free
man and not a slave, if he could write what he chose, not what he must, if
he could base his work upon his own feeling and not upon convention,
there would be no plot, no comedy, no tragedy, no love interest or
catastrophe in the accepted style, and perhaps not a single button sewn on
as the Bond Street tailors would have it. Life is not a series of gig lamps
symmetrically arranged; but a luminous halo, a semi-transparent envelope
surrounding us from the beginning of consciousness to the end.[25]

An ordinary mind on an ordinary day—add an ordinary life and
you have the given characteristics of Mary Lavin's stories. What
transforms this world into an extraordinary aesthetic experience is
the writer's unwavering commitment to revealing the inner truths
hidden beneath the surface realities of her characters' lives. This
commitment is what Mary Lavin recognized in Katherine
Mansfield's fiction, and what she sought in her own stories. She admired Katherine Mansfield's sensitivity to experience, her genius
for seeing life in a moment, and her dedicated search for the truth.
In her most successful stories, Katherine Mansfield's perception of
the truth in some fragment of experience creates a "luminous halo"
around the moment. Her stories widen the frontiers of perception
by tracing the patterns of the buried emotion.

Driven by the same dedication to truth, Mary Lavin found a
standard in Katherine Mansfield's stories for measuring her own
success as a writer, believing that those short stories in which truth
is experienced in a flash of insight were her best efforts. "A Cup of
Tea" and "The Convert," for example, create intensely personal experiences which reveal the hidden truths of her characters' lives.
Seeing these stories as comparable to "At the Bay" and "Prelude,"
Mary Lavin believes they come closest to what she wanted to do, to
her own idea of the truth. At the other end of the scale, however,
are her stories with a pattern, those stories in which a truth is imposed upon the reader. Entertaining and clever as they often are,
stories like "The Small Bequest" and "Posy" fall short of the standard of excellence Mary Lavin found in Katherine Mansfield's fiction
and used in judging her own work.

In *The Common Reader*, Virginia Woolf also discusses the Russian influence in modern fiction. She believes that the great Russian writers understood the subjective nature of life more than any other group of writers. Their contribution to modern literature reduces much of British art to tinsel and trickery:

If we want understanding of the soul and heart where else shall we find it of comparable profundity? If we are sick of our own materialism the least considerable of their novelists has by right of birth a natural reverence for the human spirit. "Learn to make yourself akin to people. . . . But let this sympathy be not with the mind—for it is easy with the mind—but with the heart, with love towards them." In every great Russian writer we seem to discern the features of a saint, if sympathy for the sufferings of others, love towards them, endeavour to reach some goal worthy of the most exacting demands of the spirit constitute saintliness.[26]

Though Lord Dunsany does not discuss in great detail what is "reminiscent of the Russians" in Mary Lavin's early stories, he does mention that "her searching insight into the human heart and vivid appreciation of the beauty of the fields are worthy in my opinion to be mentioned beside their work."[27] This "searching insight into the human heart" is the thread which draws together Virginia Woolf, Katherine Mansfield, and Mary Lavin and unites them with the Russian writers. An "understanding of the soul and heart" and "a natural reverence of the human spirit" are what most characterize the best stories of Virginia Woolf, Katherine Mansfield, and Mary Lavin.

One obvious influence on Mary Lavin's fiction is the work of Ivan Turgenev. "An Akoulina of the Irish Midlands," it has been noted, is a retelling of Turgenev's "The Tryst." Though only a few of her stories use the first-person narrative of *A Sportsman's Sketches*, her short fiction shares the same tender and sympathetic vision as Turgenev's. Her "An Akoulina of the Irish Midlands" suffers by comparison to "The Tryst" because it is more contrived in execution, but in Mary Lavin's best fiction she shares Turgenev's depth of understanding of the world of character and feeling. Both writers, working within a familiar and ordinary world, create a vision of the larger pattern of human nature out of their characters' small intimacies and failures. Free of the usual emphasis on plot, their stories reveal a hidden world in which folly and endurance, wonder and despair, exist within what Henry James, in describing the work of Turgenev, called "an exquisite envelope of poetry," a phrase similar to Virginia Woolf's "luminous halo." James's description of *A Sportsman's Sketches* is applicable to Mary Lavin's best collections, but particularly to *Tales from Bective Bridge* and *In the Middle of the Fields:*

The tenderness, the humor, the variety of *A Sportsman's Sketches* revealed on the spot an observer with rare imagination. These faculties had attached themselves, together, to small things and to great: to the misery, the simplicity, the piety, the patience, of the unemancipated peasant; to all the natural wonderful life of earth and air and winter and summer and field and forest; to queer apparitions of country neighbors, of strange local eccentricities; to old-world practices and superstitions; to secrets gathered and types disinterred and impressions absorbed. . . .[28]

While Mary Lavin shares a common vision with Turgenev, her fiction is equally indebted to the work of Anton Chekhov. She has been influenced by Chekhov's genius for placing emphasis on gestures, words, moods, and situations which seem to have no immediate relevance until they suddenly reveal some hidden meaning or secret truth. Her stories also closely resemble Chekhov's in their use of provocative moods as a substitute for conventional plotting. Not only does she share Chekhov's interest in lives which appear narrow and drab on the surface, she has the same tendency to act as a detached observer even though she obviously has sympathy and compassion for her characters.

Mary Lavin's stories often have the same type of character, situation, and movement as Chekhov's "The Kiss." Ryabovich, who describes himself as the most modest and most undistinguished officer in his whole brigade, encounters the most extraordinary experience of his life when he accidentally receives a kiss intended for another. Out of this one moment, he creates a dreamworld in which the kiss becomes the symbol of love, marriage, and family. Only when he returns to the scene of the kiss does Ryabovich recognize the absurdity of his vision and the mediocrity of his life. In her unpublished notes, Mary Lavin jotted down in two different places Thomas Mann's praise of Chekhov's genius as a short-story writer, particularly his ability to embrace the fullness of life within the limitations of the short form of fiction and to raise that medium to an epic level. In "The Kiss" Chekhov achieves this fullness by using the incident of the kiss as a way of revealing Ryabovich's secret loneliness. In a more conventional short story the unexpected kiss could easily have been a clever and comic ending to a rather entertaining story. But in Chekhov's story, the incident serves the larger purpose of exposing Ryabovich's barren life. With the emphasis on character rather than plot, the story becomes an extraordinary revelation of the hidden emotional currents of even this most commonplace individual. The Ryaboviches, Belikovs, and Alyohins have little to recommend them beyond the sensitive genius and sympathetic heart of their creator. Rarely attractive, they seem, nevertheless, much closer to humanity than the more conventional heroes of fiction.

Mary Lavin possesses Chekhov's sympathetic genius for portraying common humanity. In story after story she reveals the terrible loneliness of the shy and timid. While her narrative exposes the tragic circumstances of individuals caught in domestic situations which force them to act meanly and cruelly, the focus is always upon the twisted and tormented humanity of her characters. The most frightened, the most timid, even the most repulsive characters, have the chance to tell their own stories, reveal their own failures or empty triumphs. The Agnes Hollands, Manny Ryans, Mona Clanes, and Vera Traskes all come to life because of Mary Lavin's commitment to the truth of their experiences. Once her subject matter is established, she creates a world extraordinary in its revelation of the emotions hidden in common and undistinguished lives.

Chekhov's approach in "The Kiss," of exposing Ryabovich's secret hopes and frustrations through an unexpected external event, is the same basic strategy Mary Lavin has used throughout her career. One of the most typical situations in her stories is the sudden encounter with death. In this type of story, her character's routine existence is so disturbed by the experience that he has difficulty returning to the normal pattern of his life. In "The Cemetery in the Demesne," a carter who enjoys company and loves to tell a good story becomes uncharacteristically silent and hostile after his strange meeting with a lonely woman and her dying child. The young boy in "The Living" feels differently about life and death after his first opportunity to see a dead person. Stories as outwardly different as "The Will," "A Tragedy," and "The Convert" have the same basic emotional pattern. In each case, death forces a character to recognize the truth of his feelings or lack of feelings for another human being.

In "A Will" and "The Convert," the presence of death reveals the lack of compassion in the world of the living. The death of the

154

MARY LAVIN

mother in "The Will" exposes the resentment and social embarrassment the Conroy family has suffered because of Lally's poverty.
Only Lally retains some emotional dignity by rejecting the family's
offer of charity. In "The Convert," Elgar's unhappy life with
Mamie surfaces briefly when he reacts so strongly to the death of
Naida Paston. Trapped into marriage by his own passions, Elgar has
to live with the consequences of his disastrous decision to follow his
desires rather than his finer instincts. "A Tragedy" follows the same
pattern as "The Kiss." Mary's divided emotional loyalty is played
out against the background of the plane crash. On the surface, the
national tragedy is the major event of the story. In terms of the
relationships between Mary, Tom, and Sis, however, it functions as
a catalyst, bringing Mary face to face with the truth of her life with
Sis and Tom.

Death plays a more complex role in Mary Lavin's widow stories.
Rather than briefly disturbing the normal pattern of things, death
becomes an inextricable part of her characters' lives. Interwoven
with problems of time and memory, death forces her widows to
accept their emotional isolation as part of a painful search for self-
identity. "In a Café" and "In the Middle of the Fields" observe
widows still struggling with the painful memories of their husbands'
deaths. The widow of "In the Middle of the Fields" has yet to overcome her feelings of emptiness and senseless longing. Because these
feelings are bound together with thoughts of her husband, her
memories plague her efforts to overcome her grief. "In a Café"
observes the moment of recovery for the widow. She passes through
a personal crisis that releases her from the crippling emotions
associated with her husband's death. For the first time, she learns to
accept her grief as an undeniable part of her past. Thus memory,
which brings so much involuntary grief and suffering, is also the
potential source of a new and independent life.

In "The Cuckoo-spit" Mary Lavin fully explores the difficult
passage from grief and loneliness to emotional well-being. Though
Vera's May-September love affair ends before it ever really begins,
she gains some insight into the full range of emotions associated
with the memories of her past life with her husband. Already knowing the terrible pain of love, she now remembers its simple joys and
pleasures. Even as she rejects a love affair with Fergus as physically
impossible, she comes out of their brief encounter with the balanced
emotional state she so desperately needs to recover her self-identity
and continue her life.

III   *Mary Lavin and Sarah Orne Jewett*

Out of all the literary influences on her work, Mary Lavin has made a special point of acknowledging her debt to Sarah Orne Jewett. On the surface, the literary relationship is a strange one—an ignored writer recognizing the genius of a forgotten writer, an Irish writer without strong nationalistic themes responding to an American writer who etches the delicate patterns of a seaside town in Maine. Several keys to Mary Lavin's appreciation of Sarah Orne Jewett, however, are in Willa Cather's preface to *The Best Stories of Sarah Orne Jewett.* At one point in her unpublished notes on the short story, Mary Lavin mentions Willa Cather's interest in Sarah Orne Jewett's work. In discussing the absolute importance of truth in fiction, she recalls Willa Cather's comment that Sarah Orne Jewett was satisfied with being slight if she could be true. This is one of several judgments made in the preface that apply as well to the stories of Mary Lavin. Willa Cather begins with an observation from a Sarah Orne Jewett letter: "The thing that teases the mind over and over for years, and at last gets itself put down rightly on paper—whether little or great, it belongs to literature."[29] For Willa Cather, this remark summarizes the art of Sarah Orne Jewett's fiction. Her stories belong to the tradition of great literature because they have emerged out of the persistently recurring patterns of her mind. The design of her stories "is, indeed, so happy, so right, that it seems inevitable; the design is the story and the story is the design."[30]

These opening statements have an obvious relevance to Mary Lavin's fiction. The recurrent patterns of emotional conflict, the sudden revelation of the secret truths of lonely human beings, suggest that her work has gone through the same "teasing" process described by Sarah Orne Jewett. Her repeated use of the landscape and characters of Castlerampart also suggests that she is reworking the raw materials of her experiences into certain imaginative patterns of art much in the manner of Faulkner, Joyce, and, of course, Sarah Orne Jewett. As for the Jamesian needle and thread, except for an occasionally intrusive narrative comment, Mary Lavin's stories maintain a remarkable balance of form and content. Her point of view is strategically controlled from the perspective of the central character, thereby creating an interdependence of form (character's view) and content (character's movements, feelings, and discoveries).

After describing the virtue of Sarah Orne Jewett's fiction, Willa
Cather takes up the question of reputation. She notes that a "great
many good stories were being written upon New England themes at
the same time that Miss Jewett was writing; stories that to many
contemporary readers may have seemed more interesting than hers,
because they dealt with more startling 'situations,' were more heavily accented, more elaborately costumed and posed in the studio."[31]
Whatever immediate interest these stories created, they faded into
obscurity because they lacked "the one thing that survives all
arresting situations, all good writing and clever story-
making—inherent, individual beauty."[32] A writer achieves this individual sense of beauty by devoting himself to his art, by developing his capacity to sympathize into a rare creative gift:

The artist spends a life-time in loving the things that haunt him, in having
his mind "teased" by them in trying to get these conceptions down on
paper exactly as they are to him and not in conventional poses supposed to
reveal their character; trying this method and that, as a painter tries
different lightings and different attitudes with his subject to catch the one
that presents it more suggestively than any other. And at the end of a
lifetime he emerges with much that is more or less happy experimenting,
and comparatively little that is the very flower of himself and his genius.[33]

Very early in her career Mary Lavin knew that her stories did not
have the startling situations that immediately attract attention.
Even her admirers were advising her to use more plot and stronger
conclusions in her stories. Her response to the criticism was "A
Story with a Pattern." She accomplished two purposes in writing
this story. On the one hand, she showed with the tale of Murty
Lockwood that she was quite capable of writing a story with a
"meaty" plot and ending. The real story, however, is the debate
between the writer and her well-meaning critic. Confronted with
this impressive story with a pattern, the writer still keeps her faith in
her own approach to her work, arguing that life has little plot and is
not rounded off at the edges. Mary Lavin's early stories from "Miss
Holland" to "A Happy Death" generally support the writer's point
of view in "The Story with a Pattern." In these stories, she achieved
a high degree of success by devoting herself to the truth without
any concession to literary conventions. Unfortunately, possibly
because her early stories received little critical attention, she turned
to writing a more conventional short story at about the time of the

publication of "A Story with a Pattern." Immediately interesting
and entertaining, these stories lack "inherent, individual beauty."

Mary Lavin returned to her own vision of art with her widow
stories. Those tales of love lost and grief endured represent her best
work. *In the Middle of the Fields* is perhaps the best single group of
Lavin stories ever published, the one upon which her reputation
should finally rest. "In the Middle of the Fields," "The Cuckoo-
spit," and "One Summer" all have that happy balance of representative subject matter and intrinsic form. Even the dark and powerful "The Mock Auction," which at first seems so out of character
with the rest of her fiction, shines forth with its own particular
quality of beauty out of the squalor and misery endured by its central character. Among the stories in her later collections, "Happiness", "The Lost Child," "Asigh," and "A Memory" continue
the pattern of excellence begun with *Tales from Bective Bridge* and
resumed with *In the Middle of the Fields.*

Willa Cather's preface contains several other views of Sarah Orne
Jewett which apply to Mary Lavin, but the stories themselves also
offer some insight into Mary Lavin's fiction. Not only do the stories
of Sarah Orne Jewett and Mary Lavin share a common vision, they
also reflect a mutual interest in shy, lonely, and disappointed
human beings who still manage to retain some quiet dignity in the
face of their defeat. Two of the most interesting cases in *The Country of the Pointed Firs* are Joanna Todd and Abby Martin. Joanna
Todd is a character right out of the pages of Nathaniel Hawthorne's
fiction. A kindred spirit of Goodman Brown and Ethan Brand, she
endures a self-imposed exile on Shell-heap Island because of an unhappy love affair. Her reason for becoming the only human inhabi-
tant of the island is not revenge for being crossed in love but
"punishment" for committing the unpardonable sin: "I was in
great wrath and trouble, and my thoughts was so wicked towards
God that I can't expect ever to be forgiven. I have come to know
patience, but I have lost my hope."[34] She becomes one of those
hauntingly reclusive characters in fiction that trouble the mind and
heart because they accept such a terrible responsibility for their disappointment and sorrow.

Abby Martin compensates for her great loneliness by taking an
avid interest in Queen Victoria. Born on the same day as Victoria,
she is known in the village as the Queen's Twin. In spite of the
hardships of land, climate, and age, her character and manners have
a nobility and beauty that make her the Queen's Twin in more than

coincidence and interest. Also possessed of a rare imagination and a sensitive heart, she seems to have some mystical kinship with the ancient Nature deities. Out of the cast of characters in *The Country of the Pointed Firs,* the story of Abby Martin best exemplifies the quiet and delicate art of Sarah Orne Jewett. Absent of any startling situation and clever twists of fate, the narrative of her simple life nevertheless shines forth with a truth and clarity Mary Lavin admired and sought in her own fiction.

Throughout the Lavin canon there are a number of carefully drawn studies of sensitive, timid souls who cannot accept the harsh realities of life and, like the Joanna Todds and Abby Martins, work out what Augustine Martin calls "a cool cloistered compromise."[35] Henry Bromell believes that Mary Lavin's "portraits of 'obscure destinies' are more understanding than most of Joyce's in *Dubliners,* less sentimental than Sherwood Anderson's in *Winesburg, Ohio.* She has what Willa Cather, speaking of Katherine Mansfield, called 'the gift of sympathy'—a talent, it could be argued, essential to the art of the short story."[36] Her portraits of sensitive individuals whose frustrated and lonely lives are exposed through some confrontation with a less sensitive, more vital character reflect the tragic art of Mary Lavin. The tragedy is in the failure of her feeling characters to gain some control over life, while her more vital characters triumph even though they have no compassion or understanding for others. Countering this tragic view, however, is Mary Lavin's later vision of life as the only chance for love and happiness in spite of its many deceptions and traps. Once, when asked to draw a self-portrait, Mary Lavin submitted a two-headed stick figure of a woman, one head frowning in the midst of a downpour, the other smiling in response to the sensory appeal of nature.[37] Though hardly prize-winning, the portrait is a simple expression of her tragicomic vision of a life full of bitter experiences, but well worth the living.

The magic of Mary Lavin's art is in her genius for creating the experience of perceptual and emotional truth out of the commonplace realities of her characters. Though believing that Mary Lavin is not as subtle as Chekhov or as brilliant as Katherine Mansfield, Bromell, whose brief essay is one of the most sensitive descriptions of Mary Lavin's fiction, believes that she "shares with both an uncanny ability to capture the flavor of an existence, the depths of a life's experience, within the relatively concentrated form of the short story.''[38] With her characteristic humility and her simple faith in the art of the short story, Mary Lavin could probably accept Bromell's statement, but a mention of Sarah Orne Jewett might have made her happier.

Though differing to some degree in form and content, the purpose of Mary Lavin's stories is basically the same as that of Turgenev and Chekhov as well as that of Katherine Mansfield, Sarah Orne Jewett, and Virginia Woolf. And yet her stories in their own way are as Irish as those of O'Flaherty, O'Connor, and O'Faolain. They simply reflect a people and a way of life not generally associated with Irish literature and its strongly nationalistic character. The future of Mary Lavin's reputation lies in the willingness of critics and readers to read her fiction without any preconceived notions of what to expect from an Irish writer. Those who have already done so have discovered a writer of original talent and delicate sensibility. Unfortunately, from the very beginning of her career, even the most well-meaning critics have wanted her to spoil her genius by writing stories that fit conventional formulas of the short story.

Mary Lavin has shown over the years that she is capable of writing many kinds of stories. She began her career with the type of short story which came closest to her own idea of the truth. In the middle of her career she gave her critics the story with the pattern, proving that she could answer their challenge with an entertaining, well-written story limited only by its heavy plotting and clever ending. In her widow stories, however, she returned to her own conception of the short story and wrote with a greater sympathy and understanding than ever before. Throughout her career Mary Lavin has maintained a high quality of writing in her fiction, but in early stories like "At Sallygap," "Miss Holland," "A Cup of Tea," "Sunday Brings Sunday," and "A Happy Death," she achieved the balance of form and content she admired in Chekhov, Turgenev, Katherine Mansfield, and Sarah Orne Jewett. In later stories, particularly "In a Café," "In the Middle of the Fields," "The Cuckoospit," "The Lost Child," and "A Memory," she brought a new depth to her fiction. These stories alone are worthy of the careful reading and serious study given to the best short stories of modern literature.

Mary Lavin's stories have had little influence on contemporary Irish fiction. But if young Irish writers in the future heed Yeats's

parting advice to "learn your trade,| Sing whatever is well made,"
then they are bound to turn to her fiction as an example of "well
made" Irish art. Indeed, if her stories drift further and further into
critical obscurity, she will have suffered the sort of literary tragedy
that has befallen other woman writers of genius and vision, including Sarah Orne Jewett and Willa Cather. So many of Mary
Lavin's characters suffer a lonely and bitter existence because they
find no outlet for their feelings. While Mary Lavin has overcome
the bitterness and frustration of her personal and professional life, it
is still important that this artist of the shy, the lonely, the trapped
individual not suffer the neglect endured by many of her characters.
Like Miss Holland, she has remained steadfast in her commitment
to the truth. Mary Lavin's stories now invite the sensitive and understanding reader to experience that truth in her fiction.

Notes and References

Chapter One

1. "Writer at Work: An Interview with Mary Lavin," *St. Stephen's* (Trinity Term, No. 12, 1967), p. 22.
2. Most of the material in this chapter was discussed with Mary Lavin at the Abbey Farm, Bective. She generously provided information and clarified contradictions and misinformation that appear in other biographical sources.
3. Mary Lavin, "Tom," *New Yorker*, 48 (January 20, 1973), p. 34.
4. "Tom," p. 34.
5. Mary Lavin, "Lemonade," *The Great Wave and Other Stories* (New York, 1961), p. 78.
6. Mary Lavin, *A Likely Story* (New York, 1957), pp. 1 - 2.
7. "Writer at Work: An Interview with Mary Lavin," p. 20.
8. Ibid.
9. Ibid.
10. For a detailed discussion of Mary Lavin's literary relationship with Seumas O'Sullivan and Lord Dunsany see Robert W. Caswell, "Mary Lavin: Breaking a Pathway," *Dublin Magazine*, 6 (1957), pp. 32 - 44.
11. Lord Dunsany, "A Preface," *Tales from Bective Bridge* (Boston, 1942), p. xii.
12. Those comments, summarized here, are from unpublished papers in the Mary Lavin collection at Southern Illinois University, Carbondale.
13. Mary Lavin, "Preface," *Selected Stories* (New York, 1959), p. vii.
14. The comments by Edward Weeks appear in "The Peripatetic Reviewer," *Atlantic Monthly*, 204 (August 1959), p. 78 - 79.
15. Mary Lavin, *Happiness and Other Stories* (London, 1969), p. 11.

Chapter Two

1. Robert W. Caswell, "Irish Political Reality and Mary Lavin's *Tales from Bective Bridge*," *Eire-Ireland*, 3 (Spring 1968), pp. 53 - 54.
2. For a detailed discussion of the parallels between "At Sallygap" and "A Little Cloud" see Robert W. Caswell, "The Human Heart's Vagaries," *Kilkenny Review*, 12 - 13 (Spring 1965), pp. 77 - 82.
3. Mary Lavin, *Tales from Bective Bridge* (Boston, 1942), p. 98. All subsequent quotations from stories in the collection are taken from this edition.

4. For an entire chapter devoted to contrasting characters see Bobbie Jean Roark, *Mary Lavin: The Local and the Universal,* Dissertation, University of Colorado, 1968.

5. Augustine Martin, "A Skeleton Key to the Stories of Mary Lavin," *Studies,* 52 (Winter 1963), p. 403.

6. This view is held in Bobbie Jean Roark's dissertation. See also C. A. Murphy's chapter on Mary Lavin in *Imaginative Vision and Story Art in Three Irish Writers, Sean O'Faolain, Mary Lavin, and Frank O'Connor,* Dissertation, Trinity College, Dublin, 1968.

7. Mary Lavin, "Preface," *Selected Stories* (New York, 1959), p. vii.

8. Ibid.

9. Zack Bowen, *Mary Lavin* (Lewisburg, Pa., 1975), p. 54.

10. Mary Lavin, *The Long Ago and Other Stories* (London, 1944), p. 21. All subsequent quotations from stories in the collection are taken from this edition.

11. Mary Lavin, *The Becker Wives and Other Stories* (London, 1946), p. 76. All subsequent quotations from stories in the collection are taken from this edition.

12. *Mary Lavin,* p. 36.

Chapter Three

1. Mary Lavin, "Preface," *Selected Stories* (New York, 1959), vii.

2. Ibid.

3. From the Mary Lavin collection at Southern Illinois University, Carbondale.

4. Mary Lavin, *The House in Clewe Street* (Boston, 1945), p. 13. All subsequent quotations will be taken from this edition.

5. Zack Bowen, *Mary Lavin* (Lewisburg, Pa., 1975), p. 59.

6. Two chapters, "Bart and Ellie" and "Rosie and Frank," are named after the key relationship in the chapter. The last chapter, "Mary and Rosie," is named after mother and daughter.

7. Mary Lavin, *Mary O'Grady* (Boston, 1950), p. 18. All subsequent quotations will be taken from this edition.

8. "Preface," p. vii.

Chapter Four

1. Mary Lavin, *A Single Lady and Other Stories* (London, 1951), p. 76. All subsequent quotations from stories in the collection are taken from this edition.

2. Robert W. Caswell, "Mary Lavin: Breaking a Pathway," *Dublin Magazine,* 6 (1967), p. 42.

3. Ibid.

4. The statements appear in the notes for an essay on the short story that are a part of the unpublished papers in the Mary Lavin collection at Southern Illinois University, Carbondale.

5. Katherine Mansfield, *The Short Stories of Katherine Mansfield* (New York, 1937), p. 553.

6. *The Short Stories of Katherine Mansfield*, p. 350.

7. Mary Lavin, *The Patriot Son and Other Stories* (London, 1956), p. 91. All subsequent quotations from stories in this collection are taken from this edition.

8. Frank O'Connor, *The Lonely Voice: A Study of the Short Story* (New York, 1962), p. 203.

9. Castlerampart, the fictional counterpart of Athenry, seems to be the basic setting for most of the stories in *The Patriot Son*.

10. The narrator in "An Akoulina of the Irish Midlands" is more active and intrusive than the narrator in Turgenev's "The Tryst." Because of this interference, Mary Lavin's story is a weak and contrived version of Turgenev's.

11. Augustine Martin, "A SkeletonKe6uto the Stories of Mary Lavin," *Studies*, 52 (Winter 1963), p. 398.

12. Mary Lavin, *The Great Wave and Other Stories* (New York, 1961), p. 154.

13. Ibid, p. 165.

14. Ibid, p. 174.

Chapter Five

1. Mary Lavin, *The Great Wave and Other Stories* (New York, 1961), p. 7. All subsequent quotations from stories in the collection are from this edition.

2. Zack Bowen, *Mary Lavin* (Lewisburg, Pa., 1975), p. 34.

3. Mary Lavin, *In the Middle of the Fields and Other Stories* (London, 1967), p. 9. All subsequent quotations from stories in the collection are from this edition.

4. Mary Lavin, *Happiness and Other Stories* (London, 1969), p. 15. All subsequent quotations from stories in the collection are from this edition.

5. *Mary Lavin*, p. 42.

6. Mary Lavin, *A Memory and Other Stories* (London, 1972) p. 9. All subsequent quotations from stories in the collection are from this edition.

7. Summary of a statement made by Mary Lavin in an unpublished interview with Zack Bowen.

Chapter Six

1. Benedict Kiely, *Modern Irish Fiction—A Critique* (Dublin, 1950), p. 57.

2. Lord Dunsany, "A Preface," *Tales from Bective Bridge* (Boston, 1942), p. xi.

3. Frank O'Connor, *The Lonely Voice: A Study of the Short Story* (New York, 1962), p. 211.

4. V. S. Pritchett, "Introduction," *Mary Lavin: Collected Stories* (Boston, 1971), pp. xii - xiii.
5. Augustine Martin, "A Skeleton Key to the Stories of Mary Lavin," *Studies*, 52 (Winter 1963), p. 393.
6. Ibid.
7. Robert W. Caswell, "Irish Political Reality and Mary Lavin's *Tales From Bective Bridge*," *Eire-Ireland*, 3 (Spring 1968), p. 59.
8. Zack Bowen, *Mary Lavin* (Lewisburg, Pa., 1975) p. 23.
9. Ibid., pp. 71 - 72.
10. *The Lonely Voice*, p. 203.
11. Ibid., p. 204.
12. Thomas J. Murray, "Mary Lavin's World: Lovers and Strangers," *Eire-Ireland*, 7 (1972), p. 125.
13. Ibid.
14. Ibid., p. 131.
15. "A Skeleton Key to the Stories of Mary Lavin," p. 397.
16. *Modern Irish Fiction*, p. 93.
17. "Writer at Work: An Interview with Mary Lavin," *St. Stephen's* (Trinity Term, No. 12, 1967), p. 22.
18. Ibid.
19. Mary Lavin, "Preface," *Selected Stories* (New York, 1959), p. v.
20. Ibid., p. vi.
21. Ibid., p. vii.
22. Ibid.
23. Ibid.
24. Ibid., p. viii.
25. Virginia Woolf, *The Common Reader* (New York, 1953), p. 154.
26. Ibid., pp. 157 - 58.
27. "A Preface," p. ix.
28. Henry James, "Ivan Turgénieff," in *The Portable Henry James*, edited by Morton Dauwen Zabel, (New York, 1962), p. 459.
29. Willa Cather, "Preface," *The Best Stories of Sarah Orne Jewett*, Vol. I (Cambridge: 1925), p. ix.
30. Ibid., p. x.
31. Ibid.
32. Ibid., p. xi.
33. Ibid., p. xii.
34. *The Best Stories of Sarah Orne Jewett*, Vol. I, p. 121.
35. "A Skeleton Key to the Stories of Mary Lavin," p. 403.
36. Henry Bromell, "Mary Lavin: A Note," *Ploughshares*, Special Fiction Issue, 3 (1976), p. 31.
37. *Self-Portrait: Book People Picture Themselves*, From the Collection of Bart Britton, (New York, 1976), p. 212.
38. "Mary Lavin: A Note," p. 31.

Selected Bibliography

PRIMARY SOURCES

At Sallygap and Other Stories. Boston: Little, Brown, 1947.
The Becker Wives and Other Stories. London: Michael Joseph, Ltd., 1946.
Collected Stories. Introduction by V. S. Pritchett. Boston: Houghton Mifflin, 1971.
The Great Wave and Other Stories. New York: Macmillan, 1961.
Happiness and Other Stories. London: Constable, 1969.
The House in Clewe Street. Boston: Little, Brown, 1945; London: Michael Joseph, Ltd., 1945. Serialized earlier under the title of *Gabriel Galloway* in *Atlantic Monthly*, CLXXIV (November 1944), 155 - 64; (December 1944), 159 - 68; CLXXV (January 1945), 125 - 40; (February 1945), 139 - 48; (March 1945), 139 - 48; (April 1945), 143 - 52; (May 1945), 139 - 48.
In the Middle of the Fields and Other Stories. London: Constable, 1967; New York: Macmillan, 1969.
A Likely Story, New York: Macmillan, 1957; Dublin: Dolmen Press, 1967.
The Long Ago and Other Stories. London: Michael Joseph, Ltd., 1944.
Mary O'Grady, Boston: Little, Brown, 1950; London: Michael Joseph, Ltd., 1950.
A Memory and Other Stories. London: Constable, 1972; Boston: Houghton Mifflin, 1973.
The Patriot Son and Other Stories. London: Michael Joseph, Ltd., 1956.
The Second-Best Children in the World. Boston: Houghton Mifflin, 1972.
Selected Stories. Preface by author. New York: Macmillan, 1959.
A Single Lady and Other Stories. London: Michael Joseph, Ltd., 1951.
The Stories of Mary Lavin. Vols. 1, 2. London: Constable, 1964, 1974.
Tales from Bective Bridge. Preface by Lord Dunsany. Boston: Little, Brown, 1942; London: Michael Joseph, Ltd., 1943.

SECONDARY SOURCES

BOWEN, ZACK. *Mary Lavin.* Lewisburg: Bucknell University Press, 1975. Part of the Irish Writers Series, James F. Carens, General Editor. Contains valuable biographical information. Also has chapters on major themes, basic methods, and the two long novels. A fine guidebook for readers interested in Mary Lavin's best fiction.
BROMELL, HENRY. "Mary Lavin: A Note." *Ploughshares*, Special Fiction

Issue, 3 (1976), 30 - 32. A sensitive comment on Mary Lavin's fictional world and her place in the history of the modern short story.

CASWELL, ROBERT W. "The Human Heart's Vagaries." *Kilkenny Review*, 12 - 13 (Spring 1965), 69 - 89. The first of three essays written by Caswell on Mary Lavin's fiction and career. It focuses on the demands made by the emotional complexities of the short stories.

———. "Irish Political Reality and Mary Lavin's *Tales from Bective Bridge.*" *Eire-Ireland*, 3 (Spring 1968), 48 - 60. Contends that *Tales from Bective Bridge* is as important if not as influential as Moore's *The Untilled Field*, Joyce's *Dubliners*, and O'Flaherty's *Spring Sowing*.

———. "Mary Lavin: Breaking a Pathway." *Dublin Magazine*, 6 (1967), 32 - 44. A study of Mary Lavin's early literary relationships with Seumas O'Sullivan and Lord Dunsany. Carefully establishes the specific contributions made by the earliest admirers of Mary Lavin's short stories, and offers some interesting insight into Dunsany's true role in Mary Lavin's early career.

DUNSANY, LORD. "A Preface." *Tales from Bective Bridge*. Boston: Little, Brown, 1942, vii - xiii. In this noteworthy essay, Dunsany acknowledges Mary Lavin's special talent for realism. What is particularly remarkable in Dunsany's preface is his willingness to offer his unqualified support for a new writer. There is a vague but well intended comparison between Mary Lavin's stories and the work of the Russian writers.

MARTIN, AUGUSTINE. "A Skeleton Key to the Stories of Mary Lavin." *Studies*, 52 (Winter 1963), 393 - 406. An outstanding introduction to Mary Lavin's short stories. Correctly evaluates her as more of a European than an Irish artist in outlook. Martin's essay offers the first recognition and critical analysis of the Grimes stories.

MURPHY, C. A. *Imaginative Vision and Story Art in Three Irish Writers, Sean O'Faolain, Mary Lavin, and Frank O'Connor*. Dissertation. Trinity College, Dublin, 1968. Justification for thesis on these three Irish writers is their similarities of background, experience, and accomplishment—particularly their treatment of the Irish middle class and their use of the realistic conventions of the short story.

MURRAY, THOMAS J. "Mary Lavin's World: Lovers and Strangers." *Eire-Ireland*, 7 (1972), 122 - 31. Murray believes that readers will have trouble accepting the cheapness and meanness of Mary Lavin's characters. He does, however, praise her objectivity and the absence of imposed truths and clichés about "Irishness" in many of her short stories.

O'CONNOR, FRANK. "The Girl at the Gaol Gate." *A Review of English Literature*, 1 (April 1960), 25 - 33. Later published as a chapter in *The Lonely Voice: A Study of the Short Story*. Cleveland and New York: World, 1963, pp. 202 - 211. A rambling study of several of Mary Lavin's stories that suffers from its lack of a clear perspective. It is, however, a valuable essay because it shows the difficulty of evaluating the Lavin canon from the rigid viewpoint of the Irish Literary Renaissance.

PRITCHETT, V. S. "Introduction." *Collected Stories.* Boston: Houghton Mifflin, 1971, ix - xiii. Pritchett's introduction follows the direction first suggested by Dunsany. It compares Mary Lavin's stories to those of the Russian writers, though it limits her range to that of Leskov, Aksakov, or Shchedrin rather than Turgenev or Tolstoy.

ROARK, BOBBIE JEAN. *Mary Lavin: The Local and the Universal.* Dissertation. University of Colorado, 1968. This long study stresses the universal appeal of Mary Lavin's themes and their development within limited portrayals of character and situation. There are chapters on the themes of death and bereavement, imprisonment, contrasting characters, and love and marriage.

Index

(The works of Mary Lavin are listed under her name)